W9-BBA-757

THE PHILIPPINE ANSWER
TO COMMUNISM

THE REPUBLIC OF THE PHILIPPINES (*Inset*) AND THE ISLANDS OF LUZON AND MINDANAO

The shaded area is "Huklandia," the area of the main strength of the Huk forces.

THE
PHILIPPINE ANSWER
TO COMMUNISM

Alvin H. Scaff

Stanford University Press

Stanford, California

STANFORD UNIVERSITY PRESS
STANFORD, CALIFORNIA

PUBLISHED IN GREAT BRITAIN AND INDIA
BY GEOFFREY CUMBERLEGE,
OXFORD UNIVERSITY PRESS,
LONDON AND BOMBAY

———

HENRY M. SNYDER & COMPANY, INC.
440 FOURTH AVENUE, NEW YORK 16

W. S. HALL & COMPANY
510 MADISON AVENUE, NEW YORK 22

———

———

Library of Congress Catalog Card Number: 55–9584

FOREWORD

Recent years have held little but discouragement for the peoples who cherish freedom and democracy in Asia. In Korea the stalemate of war has been followed by the stalemate of peace. After all the destruction during three years of war, Korea is still half Communist and half free. On Formosa the Chinese Nationalists face the threat of Red invasion across a narrow channel from the mainland. Internal dissension has divided the democratic Chinese forces and destroyed their effectiveness as leaders of the opposition to Red China.

In Indochina the fall of Dien Bien Phu greatly weakened the side of the allied negotiators at the Geneva Conference. The French forces have lost prestige, and confidence in the effectiveness of American aid has been shaken. For the moment the Communist forces in Malaya have been contained; but if all of Indochina falls, the land to the south will come under heavy pressure. In Indonesia the government holds office only with the support of a strong Communist minority. The Indonesian foreign policy, like that of India, has been neutralist. India's sincere efforts to preserve the peace between the East and the West have often had the effect of strengthening the Communist aggression—even perhaps encouraging it.

The picture, though gloomy, is not all dark. If Korea was not a victory, it also was not a defeat. Dien Bien Phu was an important loss, especially on the eve of the Geneva Conference, but all of Indochina still has not fallen. The independent course of Indonesia and India, though sometimes favoring the Communist cause, on other occasions has stood as a bulwark against the Communist advance.

But in one of the nations of Southeast Asia, the Philippines, the free world may take heart. Here during the past four years the young republic has made rapid progress in solving its Communist problem. This is the only place throughout the entire region where an active armed Communist rebellion has failed. This story of success is more than encouragement to the free world; it contains lessons that sorely need learning. Out of long and bitter experience the Philippines has found an answer to Communism in the combination of effective military force and constructive friendly programs. Ramon Magsaysay, as spokesman for the new policy, said in a speech delivered on Bataan Day while he was still Secretary of National Defense:

"Why is it that a foreign power has been able to trick some of our simple Filipino peasants into serving it? Let us be frank. It is because we have for too long turned our backs upon them while we satisfied our own selfish desires. However, when a persevering governmental program has been able to bridge the gap of misunderstanding and has succeeded in inspiring their confidence, and when they have become convinced that governmental authorities exercise their power as a means for their liberation, then they respond with unfailing enthusiasm and loyalty. Left to themselves, they were easy victims for the clever international swindlers who are buying men's souls with empty promises.

"Today, through EDCOR, your armed forces are proving this fact. They have said to the Huks, 'As guardians of our nation's safety, it is our duty to hunt you down and kill you if you do not surrender. But, as fellow Filipinos, we would rather help you return to a happy Filipino way of life.' Many former Huks have accepted this offer of help and today are carving out a new and good life for themselves in the lands of Mindanao.

"In this same project another great lesson in democracy is being taught the little people of our land. Working with the new settlement in friendly co-operation are members of the armed forces, demonstrating by actual deed that a democratic army is a people's army—not a club to be held over their cowering heads, but a force dedicated to the protection and welfare of every decent citizen of our Republic.

"By this policy of all-out force and all-out fellowship we are making good progress; we are fighting a winning war."

The following pages tell the story of this triumphant struggle. Emerging from the war destitute and in ruins, the Philippines has had to shoulder the tasks of reconstruction at the same time that it fought the Huks. This makes the achievement all the more impressive. The Philippines has been up against the same type of Communist-led movement—with agrarian and nationalist overtones—that has beset China, Korea, Indochina, and the other parts of Southeast Asia. As a matter of fact, the Huk war was well advanced when the Viet Minh struck in Indochina. But for a staunch defense, the Philippines might have faced in 1951 the critical situation that later threatened her sister state across the China Sea. By improving programs and eliminating mistakes, the Philippines has finally produced a formula that is based on a mature understanding of the threat of modern Communism. At a time when it is needed most, the Philippines is ready with a contribution to the free world: a victory over the Huks and a successful approach to the Communist problem in Southeast Asia. To make this experience available to all those engaged in the struggle for democracy this book is humbly dedicated.

The year of research and writing that has gone into the making of this study was made possible by a Fulbright Research Grant. For the generous support and assistance of the United States Educational Foundation in the Philippines, which is the national organization in charge of Fulbright appointees, the author wishes to express his deepest appreciation. Among the many individuals and organizations that went out of their way to dig up documents and spend hours of time relating events and explaining happenings, special credit is due the Philippine Army. The author will always remember the helpful and friendly relations with the officers in the Educational and Information Section, the Public Affairs Office, and especially the Economic Development Corps (EDCOR). With these men who have devoted themselves to the task of rehabilitating ex-Huks the author has hiked long hours through the jungle, waded through tropical rivers, and slept on bamboo slat beds, until he felt the pulse-beat of the democratic brotherhood that has turned back the Communist advance in the Philippines. Above all others the author is grateful to these Filipino friends whose efforts have so largely made it possible to write a story with a happy ending rather than an account of failure. As the years pass he will always remember the incomparable hospitality of the Filipino people, which has placed him eternally in their debt.

ALVIN H. SCAFF
Associate Professor of Sociology,
Pomona College
Fulbright Research Professor,
Philippines, 1953–54

Manila, June 1, 1954–
  Claremont, California, April 15, 1955

CONTENTS

Photographic illustrations will be found between pages 54 and 55, and pages 118 and 119.

THE PHILIPPINE ANSWER
TO COMMUNISM

CHAPTER ONE

THE HUKBALAHAP

Since its birth as an independent nation in 1946, the Philippine Republic has had to defend itself against a Communist revolt similar to those in China, Korea, Indochina, and Malaya. This has been no minor threat, no hasty uprising on the part of disgruntled hotheads, no thoughtless outbreak of terrorism by local dissidents. It has been an all-out struggle involving the Philippine Army and the Huk guerrillas, the intellectuals as well as the peasants, the residents in the metropolis and the farmers in remote villages. It has been a war of words as well as a shooting war. Its scars may be seen in the burned houses, bereaved families, bitter animosities, and political strife of the postwar Philippines.

This revolt has been organized by a Communist armed force known as the Huks, an abbreviated form of the longer word Hukbalahap (Hukbong Bayan Laban Sa Hapon), or People's Army Against the Japanese. The Huks began in the early days of the war against Japan as a guerrilla fighting force. They were by no means the only guerrilla unit in the islands, but they were the largest and most active organization in Central Luzon. After the peace with Japan in 1945 the Huks turned their efforts toward gaining control of the Philippine government through political channels. Failing in this attempt, they began a civil war in 1946. They changed their name to People's Liberation Army (Hukbong Magpalayang Bayan, or HMB), but the popular term Huk has remained in common usage.

The factors which led to the formation of the Huks run deep in the life of the country. They appear in the background and dominant interests of those who gathered in the forest of a remote barrio* in Central Luzon, March 29, 1942, to celebrate formally the beginning of the Hukbalahap. Luis Taruc, the Supremo, a wiry, persuasive, and winsome leader, came from a poor family in Pampanga; but he had managed to complete two years of pre-law training in Manila before he quit school

---

* "Barrio" is the Philippine term equivalent to village, i.e., a small cluster of houses and farms.

3

and joined the socialists in the middle of the 1930's. Taruc had been a very successful and popular organizer among the peasants. His friend, Casto Alejandrino, second in command, came from a middle-class, land-owning family which had attained some local political importance. Alejandrino was mayor of Arayat, Pampanga, at the time of the Japanese invasion. Bernardo Poblette, an older man and a socialist with a mind of his own, came to the gathering with his armed contingent of guerrilla fighters. Poblette, alias Banal, was interested only in fighting the Japanese invaders. He was a patriot; the political aims of communism never impressed him. Lino Dizon was a one-eyed, gnarled, old peasant organizer. He had never known anything but poverty and persecution. These and his remarkable native gifts as a poet and speaker endeared him to his followers. In the early days of the war he was caught by the Japanese and put to death.

A woman leader, Felipa Culala, alias Dayang-Dayang, was present with the one hundred men in her unit. She was a large woman, rough and commanding. In describing her, Taruc wrote, "Most men were afraid of her. She feared nothing."[1] Her band was fresh from a successful ambush of a Japanese patrol near the eastern edge of the Candaba Swamp, which spreads over miles of land in the heart of Central Luzon. Her men had deployed along the banks of drainage ditches in a triangle and waited until the Japanese with their Filipino puppet police walked into the trap. At close range the guerrillas opened fire. When the battle was over, they had killed nearly one hundred of the enemy and had captured thirty-eight firearms. But Dayang-Dayang, the first Huk guerrilla hero, was not destined for the kind of revolution the Communists were directing. Some months later she was liquidated. Convicted of following her own interests rather than obeying the party discipline, she was marched off and shot by a Huk firing squad.[2]

Of a radically different caliber was Vicente Lava, urbane, sophisticated, a highly educated chemist from the Bureau of Science in Manila. Lava was the Communist party's General Secretary and adviser to the Hukbalahap. He came from an aristocratic land-owning family in Bulacan Province and had completed a Ph.D. in chemistry some years before at an outstanding university in New York City.

Some of the leaders were not present at the gathering in the forest. Pedro Abad Santos, the socialist-lawyer-intellectual, had been taken into custody by the Japanese. Also captured in the early days of the occupation of Manila was Crisanto Evangelista, founder of the Philippine Communist party and an old and prominent labor leader. He had risen from the ranks in the printer's trade. At the same time and place two other party leaders were jailed. Agapito del Rosario, nephew of Abad Santos, avowed Communist and mayor of San Fernando, capital of Pampanga Province, was tortured for several months by the Japanese and then killed. Guillermo Capadocia, a labor leader who had been convicted of seditious activity as a Communist in a Supreme Court decision of 1932, suffered several months' imprisonment but was then released.

The Huk leaders from the first represented a wide variety of backgrounds. Some were men with natural ability who had risen from the ranks of the peasant organizations. Some were labor leaders and brought with them an emphasis on the "urban proletariat." Others, such as Taruc, came from poor families but had received considerable education. They had made a successful adaptation of their leadership to the peasants' interests. A few, such as Lava, were intellectuals. They thought in terms of abstract theory far above the heads of the men in the ranks, but their firm hand gave the Huk forces a direction that the sporadic peasant uprisings in the past had lacked.

Back of the leaders assembled in the forest retreat to celebrate the founding of the Huks stood the men in the ranks. They were a tattered lot: no uniforms, no insignia, and very few shoes. Their broad feet bore witness to many years of toil in the rice paddies of the lowlands; their gnarled hands gripped a variety of weapons. Some ran fingers down the barrel of a rifle; others proudly carried old-fashioned shotguns; a few had pistols. They told and retold the story of the ambush of the Japanese at the edge of the Candaba Swamp. They listened to the speeches. Old and young, they were serious and determined. These were the men who bore the burdens of the Huk guerrilla fighting.

The immediate situation, therefore, which led to the founding of the Huks was the war, with the desire to drive out the Japanese invader. But the roots of the struggle went deeper than the immediacies of war, and the Huk objectives stretched beyond the defeat of Japan to the struggle for the ultimate control of the Philippines. The Huks were no chance guerrilla organization; they were the result of a meticulously planned campaign of revolution. What was this background, and what was the organization which lay behind the Huks?

For generations the Filipino people, especially in Luzon, had expressed their dissatisfactions in revolt. The Department of Labor lists an uprising as early as 1662.[3] Another record tells of a revolt in Batangas Province in 1739. Tenants on the Jesuit estates, claiming that they had been abused and their lands taken from them, rose up and killed and burned and plundered.[4]

The history of the Philippines is spotted with many such sporadic uprisings.[5] Some of them involved anticlerical sentiment; some were primarily political and nationalistic. All of them, no matter what their stated objectives, had strong undercurrents of agrarian unrest.[6] Their mass support was drawn from the peasantry—those who had felt the pangs of poverty, the heel of landlord oppression, and the isolation of a highly centralized government which left few decisions in the hands of local communities. The peasants wanted land; they wanted schools; they wanted credit facilities that would free them from loan sharks; and they wanted a voice in government.[7] These agrarian aims had emerged from generations of experience in the rural hinterland of Luzon.

All of these uprisings, from the earliest in the seventeenth century to the Tangulan in 1931 and the Sakdals in 1935, were sporadic and poorly organized. They reflected widespread unrest among the people, but they never constituted a serious challenge to the government. None of these revolts had any direct connection with the Hukbalahap. Indirectly, they kept alive the practice of revolt: they accustomed the people to organized opposition, and they fanned the flame of agrarian unrest. But they rose, failed, and disappeared.

When the campfires of the Huk revolutionists were lighted, therefore, in the early days of the war, it was to be expected that the men who gathered, who bore the arms and did the fighting, would be the peasants. It was also in keeping with the long tradition of Philippine revolution that agrarian issues would play a prominent part in the objectives of the movement. But aside from the deep-seated unrest which made it possible for the Huks to capture the loyalties of the people and to win widespread support, the agrarian problems alone are not sufficient to explain the rise of the Huks nor the full range of their objectives. To the old issue of agrarianism must be added other factors, namely, effective organization, leadership, and a sustaining ideology. These factors, which led to a mature revolution, developed during the twenty years prior to the outbreak of hostilities with Japan. They emerge from the beginnings of Communist activity in the peasant and labor organizations of the 'twenties and the popular socialist activities during the 'thirties.

Soon after the consolidation of the Bolshevik Revolution in Russia, Communist influences appeared in the Philippines as well as in other parts of the Far East. In 1924 an American, William Janequette, invited the labor unions in Manila to send representatives to the First Congress of the Oriental Transportation Workers, to be held in Canton, China. Five delegates headed by Domingo Ponce attended the sessions, which were discovered to be Communist-organized.[8] On their return, Domingo Ponce organized a "secretariat" in Manila under the direction of the Third International of Moscow.[9] Although the precise nature of this early "secretariat" is not clear, it probably indicates the formation of a small nucleus of Communist members or sympathizers.

The next year, 1925, an invitation was extended to the Philippine Labor Congress (Congreso Obrero de Filipinas), which had been organized since 1912, to send delegates to the Red International Labor Union (RILU) meetings to be held in Canton. Among the participating organizations were the All-China Labor Federation, the Australian Council of Trade Unions, the Trade Union League of the United States, the Indonesian Labor Federation, the Confédération Géneral du Travail Unitaire Française, Nippon Rodokumai Hyegikui Tsitsy Domie, the National Minority Movement of England, the Korean Workers and Peasants Federation, the All-Russian Council of Trade Unions, and the Congreso de Obrero de Filipinas.[10] These organizations either were at that time, or were to become, the channels of Communist activity in the organized labor movement in these respective countries. This was the beginning of the period of extensive Communist infiltration in most countries throughout the world.

The invitation to this meeting was probably extended through the fabulous Mr. Tan Malacca, who arrived in Manila from Hong Kong on July 20, 1925, on board the S.S. *Empress of Russia*.[11] He misrepresented himself to the immigration officials as a Filipino and entered the country under the alias of Elias Fuentes.[12] His two-year sojourn in the islands is one of the most engaging episodes in the history of Philippine radicalism.

Being apprehended for illegal entry, Malacca claimed in the deportation hearings that he was an Indonesian nationalist sought by the Dutch government. He was a native Javanese who had been educated in Holland and who may have also studied in Moscow.[13] When he returned to Java from Europe, he was elected president of the popular nationalist Sarekat Rayat party. He claimed that Dutch spies hounded him everywhere he went. His movements took him to Sumatra, then back to Java; deported to Holland, he escaped to Asia and visited Peking, Shanghai, Canton, and Hong Kong before he finally arrived in the Philippines.

He must have been a brilliant man. Though only thirty years of age, he spoke Dutch, German, English, Malay, Javanese, and some Chinese, French, Tagalog, and Siamese. Asked about his occupation, he answered, "Making contributions to newspapers." He was president of a labor union and editor of a newspaper in Java.

Malacca's political leanings became evident in the deportation hearings. When asked about the object of the Sarekat Rayat party, he replied, "To obtain independence of the Dutch colonies by every means. . . . I believe in the action of the masses to obtain our independence by every means . . . political, economic, and if necessary physical means."

He was questioned, "What is your understanding of Bolshevism?"

Malacca: "It is a doctrine by which the laboring class of the world can achieve their social and political emancipation by uniting themselves in order to get changes in the present system by any means."

Question: "Do you subscribe to this doctrine?"

Malacca: "Theoretically, yes, but the aim must be subject to the limitations existing in each country."[14]

Malacca traveled widely in the Philippines during his stay. He made friends everywhere among labor leaders, newspapermen, and politicians. For a time he lived with Representative Ramon Torres of Negros Occidental. In Manila he was befriended by Apolinario de los Santos, president of the University of Manila, and Francisco Verona, labor leader and editor of the newspaper *El Debate*. Judge José Abad Santos served as his attorney in the deportation proceedings. Representative Claro Recto, then minority leader of the House, proposed a Tan Malacca fund. Contributions poured in.[15] Though Malacca was being deported from the Philippines, he became a political hero in the eyes of the people whose land he was forced to leave. To them he was a martyr suffering for the sake of his country's independence. In the gush of sympathy from those in high political office as well as those in the ranks of labor, no one foresaw that the ideas and convictions which Malacca had broadcast would develop through the years and bear fruit at last in the Huk rebellion.

At the first convention of the Philippine Labor Congress in May 1927, after the return of the delegates from Canton, the issue of communism was openly debated. The convention finally voted to affiliate the Philippine Labor Congress with the Red International Labor Union. The delegates also passed a resolution to organize a workers' party. Under the leadership of Evangelista and others who had become Communists, the Workers' party (Partido Obrero) was organized in 1928. Later in the year two of the men, Crisanto Evangelista and Cirilo Bognot, attended meetings in Shanghai, where they met Chou En-Lai and Earl Browder. Then they proceeded across Siberia to Moscow for training and to other conferences in Europe. They were joined in Moscow by another compatriot, Jacinto Manahan, who had made the trip alone on funds supplied by the Christintern, or Christ International, an international Communist peasant organization.[16]

On their return Evangelista reported to the Philippine Labor Congress that it had been approved as an affiliate of the Red International Labor Union. When this affiliation was publicly announced, there was a storm of protest by the press, by government officials, and by the landlords. By virtue of his studies in Moscow, Crisanto Evangelista had achieved some distinction as an authority on Russia and communism. In a series of three forum lectures at the University of the Philippines he defended the Communist position and the affiliation of the local labor organization with the Communist International.[17]

At the same time that the Communists were building up support in the organized labor unions in Manila, they also were establishing a strong beachhead among the peasant organizations of Central Luzon. The early efforts were directed largely by Jacinto Manahan, who was among the first Communists in the Philippines, but who later was discredited by the party on a charge of misuse of funds entrusted to him to send party leaders to Moscow for training.[18]

In 1919 Manahan organized the Tenants' Union of the Philippines (Unión de Aparceros de Filipinas). Three years later the union was expanded and renamed National Federation of Tenants and Agricultural Workers of the Philippines (Confederación Nacional de Aparceros y Obreros Agrícolas de Filipinas). Landlords fought the efforts of this union to secure legislation favorable to the tenants.[19] In 1924 Manahan's organization became the National Union of Peasants in the Philippines (Katipunan Pambansa ng mga Magbubukid sa Filipinas, or KPMP). It was this union which became the basis for the Communist activity among the peasants, especially in the central provinces of Bulacan and Nueva Ecija. The KPMP had a continuous existence until it merged its activities with the Huks in 1942.

In May 1929, at the convention of the Philippine Labor Congress, the Communist and the conservative leaders clashed sharply over policies and control. As a result the organization split into two factions. One body under Evangelista walked out and held its own meetings, where it was decided to organize a Congress of Philippine Workingmen (Katipunan ng mga Anak Pawis ng Filipinas). This pro-Communist meeting also voted to establish a working class party to lead the workers in their struggles for political and economic independence.[20]

During the following year a committee of Communists working with Evangelista drew up the formal documents for the new party. The constitution was approved August 26, 1930; the by-laws were adopted October 6; and the Communist party (Partido Komunista) was publicly launched in Manila on November 7, 1930. This celebration was timed to coincide with the thirteenth anniversary of the Bolshevik revolution in Russia.[21]

At the public meeting Dominador Ambrosio read the new party constitution. It contained the basic Marxist ideas of class war and the Leninist ideas of Communist party leadership. "The Philippines, as a subject nation, in order to establish an independent government has to revolt under the leadership of the laborers. . . . We need a Communist Party, one that is not reformist but revolutionary. Only by revolutionary means can we demolish the slavery of one man by another and of one nation by another nation. . . . The principal ideal of the Communist Party in the desire to head the Philippine Government is different from that of the burgess [bourgeois] political parties. Its aim is not to strengthen the capitalist government but to engender—as it cannot be avoided— the war of the classes and to bring about its downfall."[22] This was not just a local party, Communist only in name; it was real, modern communism with a Moscow connection and all the ideological trappings of Marxism and Leninism.

After the reading of the constitution, Crisanto Evangelista spoke. "He explained the advantages of the Russian Government and the means which had been employed by the laboring class of Russia to establish its present government, citing certain insurgent colonies of different nations as other examples." Pamphlets were distributed. In one of them, the manifesto of the Proletarian Union of the Philippines (Katipunan ng mga Anak Pawis sa Filipinas) was this statement: "Due to the success of Soviet Russia, revolutions were incited in the whole world. . . . The idea of revolution spreads itself, struggles become more and more serious but the labor movement continues on the path traveled by the Russian laborers—the Bolsheviks. What is that path? The seizure of the power of the government from the hands of the burgesses and the establishment of a government by the laborers."[23]

The Partido Komunista campaigned for new members vigorously and openly. Following the initial celebration, mass meetings and rallies were held almost daily for two months. The party circulated leaflets, published an official paper, *Titis* (Flame), publicly displayed its red flag with the hammer and sickle emblem, and operated a bookstore in Manila.

These activities provoked concern and opposition among civic and government leaders. The party officials found it increasingly difficult to secure permits to hold public meetings. It was this issue that brought matters to a climax and led to the outlawing of the Partido Komunista. The following account comes from the testimony which was accepted as legal evidence by the courts in the trial of the party leaders. The Communists had scheduled a May Day parade in 1931, in Caloocan, some two miles from the city limits of Manila. The permit to hold the parade was issued and then revoked. A detachment of the Constabulary proceeded to the location to see that the parade did not take place. A large crowd assembled. Crisanto Evangelista asked the Constabulary officer for permission to say a few words to the people to explain to them that the parade could not be held. "But instead of telling the people to retire, he raised his fist, which the people approved by shouting 'mabuhay' [an expression of strong approval], and then said: 'Comrades, or brethren, the municipal president, Mr. Aquino, has allowed us to hold the parade, but for reasons unknown to me, the permit has been revoked. This shows that the big ones are persecuting and oppressing us, who are small, which they have no right to do.' Then shouts were heard from the audience saying, 'Let us fight them.' The accused [in the trial] Abelardo Ramos, who was among the people, shouted, 'Let us fight them until death.' Evangelista proceeded, saying, 'My heart bleeds,' but could not continue because the officer stopped him and placed them both, Evangelista and Ramos, under arrest." The crowd advanced to rescue the leaders, but the Constabulary men dispersed them with water.[24]

Other leaders of the Partido Komunista were then arrested and brought to trial on charges of sedition and rebellion.[25] Of the twenty-seven arraigned seven were acquitted and twenty were convicted. The sentences varied in length, the longest being for eight years. The party officially was outlawed in a Supreme Court decision, October 26, 1932, and many of its leaders imprisoned, but activities continued underground and through various legal peasant and labor organizations.

During the next few years, while the Communists were suppressed, the Socialist party grew rapidly in size and influence, especially in the Central Luzon province of Pampanga. The organizer and dominant influence in this branch of the left-wing movements was a thin, emaciated ascetic named Pedro Abad Santos. He was the eldest son of a distinguished landowning family in Pampanga. His brother José was a justice of the Supreme Court at the time of the war and was one of the few high government officials to become a martyr for refusal to co-operate in the Japanese occupation government. His younger brother, Quirino Abad Santos, still living, has been a judge and a practicing attorney and a member of the Agrarian Commission of 1946.

Don Perico, as Pedro Abad Santos was familiarly called by his followers, lived a very simple life. Suffering from stomach ailments, he ate sparingly and only twice a day. He was often sick and greeted visitors from his bed. He never married, and he commented that since he had no responsibilities and few wants he was the ideal one to lead the laboring classes. Because of his ascetic tastes many referred to him as the Gandhi of the Philippines.

Though his following was large, Don Perico possessed none of the usual characteristics of the popular leader. He was not one of the common people; on the contrary, he came from the landed aristocracy. He remained at home, somewhat aloof. If people wanted to see him, they had to come to him. Don Perico applied this rule to President Quezon as well as to the lowliest peasant. The man had no commanding presence and he was a poor public speaker. In his dealings with people he was abrupt.

His college work had been interrupted by the revolution in 1896. He fought the Spanish. When the Americans came, he fought them. At the end of the fighting he was sentenced to be hanged, but the sentence was commuted to twenty-five years' hard labor. Rapidly learning English from his captors, he became valuable as an interpreter and was granted a pardon in 1903. Pedro then went back to the study of law until he passed the bar examination. In the following years he practiced law, published a paper, served two terms in the Philippine legislature, 1917–22, and visited the United States as a member of the Quezon-Osmeña Independence Commission.

Don Perico was a scholar. He read Spanish, German, Greek, Latin, and French, in addition to English and his native Pampango dialect. At one time he helped the American Bible Society translate the New Testament into the Pampango dialect. His quarters in the old family residence in San Fernando, Pampanga, were lined with books. His reading diet included the Bible in Greek, *Das Kapital* in German, the *Daily Worker* in English, and law books in various languages.[26] The peasants in Central Luzon respected and trusted him. The landlords feared and hated him; in their eyes he was a traitor to his class.

It is difficult to determine precisely when the Socialist party was started in the Philippines. Dapen Liang, the political historian, mentions a Socialist party organized by Manuel Carlos in 1916. This organization endorsed the candidacy of Isabelo de los Reyes, Martin Ocampe, Dominador Gomez, and others in the general elections of that year.[27] But this party drops out of sight and has no continuous connections with the movement led by Abad Santos. Since our problem is to trace only those organizations that had a hand in the founding of the Huks, we can dismiss these earlier efforts.

Quirino Abad Santos insists that his brother, Pedro, organized the Socialist party in 1929.[28] Since they were living in the same house at that time, his testimony must be taken seriously. The next year, according to this same source, Pedro organized the Workers and Peasants' Union (Aguman Ding Maldeng Talapegobra, or AMT). The Socialist party was conceived as an open political party for the purpose of winning voter support and elective offices. The AMT was a labor union attempting to secure better conditions and more pay for peasants and workers. The two were simply different aspects of the same movement. They included the same people, the same leaders, the same propaganda literature and promoted the same general program.

There has risen in recent years considerable argument as to whether the Socialist party of the 1930's was in truth socialist, or whether it was only a Communist party in disguise. The date of the Socialist party's origin is of importance only in connection with this debate. Interviews with men who were active in

Abad Santos' Socialist party indicate that whatever the original organizing date, the movement became active and influential and widely supported only after 1932. Prior to this time it seems safe to assume that the party existed largely on paper and in the minds and aspirations of a very small number of men around Don Perico.

[A contrary view of the beginning of the Socialist party is presented in the Communist party literature. According to José Lava, Communist party historian, Pedro Abad Santos is pictured either as a Communist himself or as a willing tool of the party to carry on the class struggle under the title of socialism as long as the Communist party was outlawed.[29] If the Lava view is correct, then the Socialist party was simply a tactic employed by the outlawed Communist party to continue the class war. The party historian without question wishes to portray this as fact. But if the opposing view is accepted, then it is possible that Pedro Abad Santos was not an actual Communist, at least in the early 1930's, and that the Socialist party had its own independent existence.

Even the Communists admit that the organizational structure of the two parties exhibited marked differences. The socialists followed a policy of open membership. Both the Socialist party and the AMT were mass organizations, unlike the highly disciplined and limited membership of the Communist party. The Communist leaders recognized these differences and traced later difficulties back to these divergent ways which characterized the groups in the 1930's.[30]

A review of what the socialists advocated and tried to accomplish should reveal whether there was any significant difference between the two parties. Those who hold that the socialists were different claim that the Abad Santos group were simply reformers. There is some evidence to support this view. For example, the Socialist party believed in the use of the ballot; they ran candidates for local offices. They employed labor union tactics to secure better working conditions for the sugar mill workers and farm tenants in Central Luzon. The socialists proposed reforms through legislation. They advocated that a law be passed which would bring about a redistribution of land in the Philippines. All holdings of over five hectares (about eleven acres) would be taken by the government and rented or resold to landless individuals in not greater than five-hectare plots. Former owners of large estates would be compensated in the form of bonds in sums totaling not more than 100,-000 pesos to each owner. These bonds would be redeemed by the government at the rate of 5 per cent a year for twenty years and at an interest rate of 2½ per cent.[31] All of this looked like a reform-type socialist program.

But this was only one side of the movement. It is also true that the Socialist party actively promoted class war. Peasants' and workers' unions held strikes, burned sugar-cane fields, held secret meetings at night, refused to vacate lands at the command of landlords, and at times met violent opposition with violent tactics. The Communists complained that the socialists were too direct and too violent. "Were the socialists correct in their liquidation of individual landlords, burning of sugar cane and rice fields, killing work animals, and utilizing threats and force to coerce people to join our organization? Comrade Evangelista took the position that such actions are terroristic and anarchist in character and violate the principles and democratic procedures followed by the party. On the other hand, Comrade Abad Santos took the position that all means which would strengthen the revolutionary forces and hasten the victory of the revolution should be utilized, and that these include the actions objected to by the Communists. He claimed that while he agrees that these actions should not be made an open policy of the party, they should be restored to as secret methods of struggle."[32]

On the other hand, Luis Taruc pictures the socialist activity in more pacific terms. In his autobiography he tells of a strike which he led in 1936. This was a sit-down strike in a stone quarry. The workers refused to leave the quarry even when a Constabulary officer threatened to run over them with a railway engine. When the officers announced that they would arrest the strikers, some of the workers reached for their tools and threatened to resist. A hurried phone call from Taruc to Don Perico brought this advice. "Try a new tactic. Let everyone be arrested." The workers marched off to jail. By the time they reached their destination they had gathered additional recruits and were a thousand strong. They overflowed the jail into the high school building. Taruc remembered the words of Don

Perico, "What the rich want is good for the rich, what the poor want is good for the poor, what the rich want the poor to do is no good for the poor. The poor must respond with unity. The poor must learn to make what they want come true. Every strike must be a school, even if it is lost." Taruc reports, "We made the strike into a school."[33]

Feeling that his political support was threatened in Central Luzon, President Quezon tried to alleviate the agrarian unrest and undercut the socialist appeal with a program of "social justice," announced in 1936. This program included the establishment of a board of arbitration to settle disputes between employers and workers, a tenancy law which would adjust relations between landlord and tenant on a fair and satisfactory basis, the acquisition of large estates at a fair price and the resale of these lands in small plots to the tenants, and the promotion of settlement on public lands in the unoccupied parts of the Philippines. But in the few years following 1936, the program of "social justice" existed largely on paper. It had no deterrent effect upon the activities of the organized peasants north of Manila. Pedro Abad Santos vigorously opposed President Quezon and his "social justice" program. He said, "We do not believe in social justice. We don't invoke social justice; we believe that if the masses have to be saved it is by their own efforts; to organize, to unite, and their only weapon is—strike. We believe that ten years of Quezon's social justice preaching would not obtain for the workers what a single good strike will accomplish for them. Father Coughlin had also been preaching social justice in America, but what he got for the workers is nothing compared to what John L. Lewis's C.I.O. has accomplished for them."[34]

In opposition to the socialist unions, the landlords promoted their own organizations. One of these, named White Stone (Batung Maputi), had as its purpose the resistance of peasant aggression by setting uniform practices in payments to tenants and by agreeing not to accept tenants who have left a landlord without "reasonable cause." Another organization begun by a group of landlords included large numbers of peasants. This was known as the Soldiers of Peace (Kawal sing Kapayapan). Used partly for political purposes, this group mustered votes for landlord candidates during elections. The primary objective of the Soldiers of Peace, who possessed some arms, was to oppose the socialists. A resident and close observer of events in Central Luzon during this time writes, "More than once did the *Kawals* clash bitterly with the socialists, resulting in the loss of lives from both parties."[35]

This class war became so violent by the middle of 1938 that President Quezon called a conference at San Fernando, Pampanga Province, to deal with the issue of peace and order. He brought with him the Secretary of Justice, the Secretary of Interior, the Secretary of Labor, the Commissioner of Public Safety, and the acting Provost Marshal General of the Philippine Army. They met with the local officials and representatives, some of whom were themselves socialists and condoned the activities of the workers and peasants. Quezon was informed that "every night at the sound of the *tambuli* [carabao horn] hundreds of laborers gathered in remote barrios, took possession of the lands where some members of the groups had been expelled, plowed and tilled the fields in spite of protests from the landowners." The president threatened to take drastic action by removing elected town mayors and appointing others in their places if the present officials did not enforce the laws and keep the peace. President Quezon said, "If I am not able to govern with elective mayors, I shall have to do so through appointive mayors. The responsibility of governing is mine and no one else's. . . . I want everybody to know my attitude. I want to govern in accordance with the will of the people. I shall respect elective officials, but if the execution of the plans of my administration is obstructed, . . . I shall have to select men who I know will help me."[36]

It was during this prewar period that the class war actually started between the Philippine government and the old political leadership, on one side, and the organized peasants and workers under Communist and socialist leadership, on the other. The issues were drawn; the organizations were formed; the leaders were identified. The same people and the same leaders who emerged from these prewar struggles on the side of the peasants and workers organized and constituted the Hukbalahap at the time of the Japanese invasion. And they were the same ones in the main who carried on the fight against the Philippine government after its independence in 1946.

As a result of the Quezon conference and the pressure from the government in Manila, permits to hold rallies and meetings were denied to the socialists in Central Luzon. They made a practice of frequenting other gatherings and seizing opportunities to promote their own program. The following is an eyewitness account of such an occasion.

"We were holding an outdoor Protestant religious meeting. The Chief of Police of that town was present at the meeting. The preacher preached on the text, 'The people which sat in darkness saw great light.' He applied these words to what happened to the Filipino people during the Spanish regime, and then subsequently during the American occupation—educationally, politically, and religiously. There was a big crowd present. Luis Taruc and other peasant agitators were also present. . . . As soon as the preacher concluded his message, Luis Taruc raised his hand and started to ask questions. His first question was, 'Since the Filipinos were enlightened educationally, politically, and religiously during the American sovereignty, were they alleviated socially and economically?' Then he continued, 'How about the oppressed tenants and the poorly paid laborers?' Without waiting for answers from the preacher, Taruc proceeded to answer his own questions; and before the Protestants could close their service, he was already delivering a fiery speech, until the Chief of Police had to whisper to the preacher that he had better close the service."[37]

How much difference was there between the socialism of the Pedro Abad Santos movement and communism? To a question on this point put to him by a newspaperman from Manila, Abad Santos once gave this reply, "There's not much difference between communism and socialism. They strive to the same end, i.e., abolition of capitalism or the profit system, and substituting instead a classless society. In methods lies the difference. Especially some years ago communism did not believe in using parliamentary methods in labor movements. It confined itself to class struggle. Socialism has always resorted to parliamentary procedure side by side with class struggle."[38]

Whether or not the socialists were really Communists disguised by a different label is really an empty question. The two were working for the same fundamental ends. The results of socialist activity in Central Luzon during the 1930's was to stir up class strife and to create a body of trained radical leaders. The men who worked with Pedro Abad Santos—Taruc, Feleo, Alejandrino, and others—became the avowed Communists and leaders of the Huks during and after World War II.

In the year 1938 the radical movement in the Philippines turned a corner. The change in events began when James Allen from the Communist party of the United States came to the Philippines and asked President Quezon to pardon the leaders of the local Communist party. The last of them, Crisanto Evangelista, was given an "absolute pardon," which meant that he was "restored to full civil and political rights," toward the end of 1938.[39] The pardons for the party leaders were made under such circumstances that they were construed as legalizing Communist party activity.[40] This impression of the legality of the Communist party was further strengthened by a series of opinions given by the Secretary of Justice to the Secretary of Labor during 1939. In effect, these decisions interpreted membership in Communist-dominated organizations and Communist activities short of open sedition as legal.[41]

Immediately after the Communist leaders were freed, negotiations began for the merger of the Communist and Socialist parties. Lava credits the American Communist party leader, James Allen, with having a hand in these arrangements. Lava writes, "There were no fundamental ideological differences between the two parties." The strongest objections to the merger appeared in the middle and lower ranks of both groups. "Some objections raised by some socialists were: (1) the Communists are Godless; (2) they are Moscow agents; (3) the KPMP [Communist peasant union] is destroying the AMT [socialist peasant union]; (4) the merger will lower the prestige of Comrade Abad Santos; and (5) the Communists are not militant."[42]

But in spite of the objections, mostly on the part of the socialists, the merger occurred. The new party was called the Communist Party of the Philippines, merger of the Communist and the Socialist Parties of the Philippines. The two peasant unions attached to the old parties (the KPMP and the AMT) were to remain separate but were to be directed by the peasant department of the new party. Various branches of the Socialist party were to be reorganized to conform to the pattern of the new union. Both parties contributed representatives to the leading committees of the merger. In some localities where the socialists had been very strong they were to supervise all party and mass organizations.[43] It took several years for the merger to be completed. Crisanto Evangelista was the first party president; Pedro Abad Santos was the vice-president; Guillermo Capadocia, a Communist convicted along with Evangelista and the others in 1932, was the first party secretary. The socialists still operated from their headquarters downstairs in the Abad Santos residence in San Fernando; the Communists set up offices across town. The war years and the guerrilla fighting completed the merging of the two groups. By the end of the war there was no Socialist party left. The Huk forces from top to bottom were welded to the Communist party leadership.

At the same convention in 1938 in which the Communists and socialists were merged, plans were made for united-front activities with other groups. The chief effort was the formation of a Frente Popular, a political party designed to attract the support of all groups left of center. Under this label the Communists were able to run two candidates for the National Assembly in the 1938 elections: Mariano P. Balgos for the north district of Manila, and Guillermo Capadocia for the south district.[44] Both men had been active in founding the Communist party; both were subsequently killed in the postwar Huk revolt.

The united-front strategy was only partly successful. The right wing of this joint effort, under the leadership of Juan Sumulong, split off and formed another Popular Front party. In the 1940 elections there were two popular-front parties demanding recognition by the Commission on Elections. Although this split undoubtedly reduced the chances of success, in Central Luzon, where the left-wing Popular Front party was strongest, Pedro Abad Santos was only narrowly defeated by Nacionalista candidate Sotero Baluyot in the Pampanga governor's race; while the socialists actually elected mayors in eight out of the twenty-one towns in the province, including the capital. Socialist or Communist mayors and councilmen had also been elected in four towns in Tarlac Province and in one place in Nueva Ecija Province.[45]

In addition to direct political action the Communists helped to organize other united-front groups: the League for the Defense of Democracy, the Youth Congress, the Congress for Democracy and Collective Security, and the Friends of China. The Congress for Democracy and Collective Security was especially active in sponsoring the boycott of Japanese goods and in arousing antifascist opinion. All of these united front activities followed the strategy of "the international proletariat."[46]

On the basis of their own political analysis the Communist leaders had concluded that the Japanese advance in Southeast Asia would engulf the Philippines. In October 1941, some two months before the first raids on the Philippines and on Pearl Harbor, the party issued orders to all cell groups to prepare for guerrilla warfare against the Japanese.[47]

By the first week in January 1942, when the Japanese entered Manila, plans had been drawn up for a Barrio United Defense Corps. This was to be a local village and town organization to keep order, to prevent looting and gangsterism, to protect crops and keep the harvest out of the hands of the Japanese, to supply the Huk fighting forces, and to resist co-operation with the Japanese.[48] The plans were written out by party leader Vicente Lava and placed on his desk top in the Bureau of Science. He put a pistol on top of them as a paperweight, expecting to return to his office for both the papers and the gun. But the quick entry of the Japanese into Manila interfered, and Lava had to flee the city. Soldiers broke into the office and took the pistol but left the papers. These were discovered a few days later by a colleague in the Bureau of Science. When he read them, he became frightened and burned them.[49] The plans, however, were soon put into effect by the Huks among its supporters in the villages.

The Communists carried on their united-front activities just so far as suited their own ends and no farther. When the Japanese invasion came, they made no effort to support the military action of the Fil-American troops. On the contrary, they assumed that the resistance to the invasion would collapse. In the early days of the fighting Pedro Abad Santos wrote a letter to General MacArthur asking him to supply arms to the people for guerrilla warfare.[50] The request, of course, was denied. The army at this time desperately needed all the arms it could command. The party leadership as always was attempting to use present opportunities to further the ultimate ends of their own revolution.

A chance meeting between Luis Taruc and an acquaintance on the morning of December 20, 1941, revealed the direction of party plans and actions. Taruc, armed with a .45 caliber pistol, was waiting at the San Fernando station for a train. The acquaintance asked if he were going to Bataan to join the Philippine Army, since they were still enlisting volunteers at this time. Taruc replied in the negative and explained that he was going to organize an army of the people right in Pampanga to check the advance of the enemy.[51] By the end of January, three months before the fall of Bataan, the nucleus of the Huk guerrilla organization had been established in Central Luzon.

The war with Japan provided the Communists with their great opportunity to move out of the stage of infiltration and tedious political maneuvering into a period of direct revolutionary activity. In the disorganization that followed on the heels of the fighting they took command. The Barrio United Defense Corps became the means of civilian control and the instrument for conduct of civilian affairs in the outlying areas. The Hukbalahap was the fighting arm. To the old issue of agrarian reform could now be added a strong plea for popular support on the basis of patriotic action against the Japanese invaders.

During this time the Huks learned how to fight a guerrilla war. From the battlefields and jungles of Bataan they retrieved enough arms to equip a guerrilla force that could challenge any but the largest Japanese occupation patrols. They learned how to hit and run, to fight for arms and ammunition, to protect the rice harvest, to build up local support, and to liquidate traitors. By their own figures the Huks claim to have killed more than 25,000 during the war, only about 5,000 of whom were Japanese.[52] The others were Filipinos whom the Huks regarded as obstructionists in the class war. Among the instructors in guerrilla tactics was a Chinese colonel from the famous Eighth Route Army of Red China. Edgar Snow's *Red Star over China* was used as a training manual.[53] When the liberation came in 1945, the Philippine government faced in Central Luzon not just an agrarian organization with a reform program, but a revolutionary movement with a trained and experienced army well equipped for guerrilla war.

In addition to its military organization the revolutionary movement had accumulated a wealth of administrative experience during the war. The Huks had controlled areas, appointed civil officials, used property, collected taxes, administered justice, and even conducted schools. These powers the Huk leaders had come to believe were theirs. They were not going to give them up without a struggle—and the struggle began almost immediately after the expulsion of the Japanese in 1945.

CHAPTER TWO

THE ARMY WITH A SOCIAL CONSCIENCE

After the liberation in 1945 the Philippines began to lift itself from the ruins of war. Manila lay prostrate, a jungle of wreckage. The old cathedrals, the legislative halls, the office buildings, the hotels, factories, homes, and shipping docks were destroyed. Sunken Japanese vessels blocked the harbor. One could stand in what had been the center of the city and look across miles of rubble. Only an occasional building had in some miraculous way escaped the bombing and shelling. In all this vast south side, where almost a million people lived, there was scarcely a family but had lost one or more of its members.

Looting and banditry made life and property unsafe. Inflation swallowed up the value of relief from abroad and reduced real earnings to a pittance. Black markets flourished. Legitimate business was much less profitable than buy-and-sell rackets.

War casualties had decimated capable leadership. Government bureaus were completely disorganized. There was no equipment, no personnel, and in many instances no records. National libraries had been destroyed. Schools opened without textbooks, without paper, and without adequate shelter from the heavy tropical rains. And yet in the midst of national disaster the people did not succumb to grief, rarely complained about their losses, and persisted in their amazing cheerfulness. Rarely have human qualities served as nobler substitutes for material wants.

Gradually some semblance of order emerged from the chaos of war. But the new order was shaky and explosive. None of the old prewar problems had disappeared; they were complicated a hundred times over by the disorganization of the war years. In this uncertain atmosphere the Philippine Republic was launched on its independent course, July 4, 1946.

The Huks also went through a period of stormy transition. Shortly after the American army landed, the Huks appointed civilian officials in the provinces and towns where they were strong. They hoped to keep these positions and use them for in-

25

creasing their power in the postwar years. The official government under Osmeña, however, disallowed the Huk claims and
appointed its own governors and mayors until elections could
be held. The United States Counter Intelligence Corps picked
up Taruc, Alejandrino, and some of the other leaders on charges
of liquidating Filipinos in disobedience to specific instructions
to cease all civil war. These men were kept in various jails and
at Iwahig Penal Colony most of the time from February 22 to
September 30, 1945. The Huk leaders were released from
prison during the period of last preparations for complete
independence. This turned out to be a costly mistake, but at the
time no one realized the full implications of the Huk conspiracy.

Haste, unavoidable though it was, led to other problems for
the new republic. Within the space of a few months' time the
United States attempted to conclude the Pacific campaign, to
grant the Philippines its independence, and to send her army
home. It is little wonder that some of the efforts were poorly
and, at times, irresponsibly administered.[1] For example, the
back-pay rackets in the Recovered Personnel Division created
one of the worst impressions of Americans during the entire
period of American-Philippine relations. While many loyal
and active guerrillas failed to receive recognition and compensation for wartime services, others who greased the palms of
finance officers or promised to work in the political machine of
ambitious guerrilla leaders tapped the generous supply of
American dollars. This generated bitterness, which the Huks
adroitly used in recruiting followers during the postwar period.

Little suspecting a full-scale Communist revolution, the
American forces were careless in the distribution of arms and
ammunition. Much that was air-dropped or passed out to guerrillas found its way into the hands of the Huks. Sympathetic
GIs traded their new weapons for old ones and souvenir pieces.
Other weapons were exchanged by hungry soldiers for fresh
fruits and poultry. Thefts from ammunition dumps carelessly
guarded were common. While the Huks were busy equipping
themselves with modern guns and plenty of new ammunition,
the newly reorganized Philippine Army at the time of independence in 1946 was supplied with war-worn hand-me-downs.

In the "Annual Report of the Chief of Staff, Armed Forces of the Philippines" it was estimated that as late as June 1948 less than 50 per cent of the materials originally promised to be turned over to the Philippine Army had actually been received. Properties which were exchanged through the agencies of the United States Foreign Liquidation Commission and the Philippine Surplus Property Commission were invariably stripped of removable fixtures and materials before the Philippine Army received them.[2] American troops had fought bravely to liberate the Philippines, but the United States Army failed dismally in not disbanding the Huks and in leaving the Philippine government weak and ill prepared to defend itself.

The Philippine Army was plagued with organizational problems. In the five months prior to independence it had to reduce its force from 132,000 men to approximately 37,000. This placed a tremendous strain on demobilization agencies and took a heavy toll on the efficiency of the fighting forces, which were divided between the Military Police Command under the Department of Interior and the Armed Forces under the Department of Defense. The largest force, 24,000 out of the total 37,000, was in the MPC, which had the responsibility for dealing with the Huk problem.[3] It took several years before the Philippines realized that the Huks were revolutionists and must be faced with an army and not just a police force.

Finding capable officers for the armed forces was especially complicated by the collaborationist issue. Before an officer could be assigned for duty he had to be cleared of any charges. What constituted collaboration? The question was never given a workable and definitive answer; but while it was being debated in the courts and commissions and political circles, the army suffered from insufficient personnel.

Ultimately, practically all individuals were cleared regardless of the degree of their co-operation with the enemy. Yet, in the years right after the war, resentment against collaboration was still strong. The fact that the first president of the Philippine Republic, Manuel Roxas, and many of his men in government offices had held offices under the Japanese gave the Huks a ready talking point in their antigovernment drive. Many of the soldiers and officers in the Military Police Command charged with the elimination of the Huks had served in the

Bureau of Constabulary under the Japanese.[4] Others had long been identified with the opposition to the peasant movements in Central Luzon. General Rafael Jalandoni, Chief of Staff of the new Armed Forces, had been the major of the Philippine Constabulary who arrested Evangelista and Capadocia in a public meeting in May 1931 on charges of sedition and illegal association. With such old and deep-seated antagonisms aroused, no harmonious end to the fighting was possible.

The new Roxas administration claimed that it would wipe out the Huks in sixty days. Extermination through military action was the basic aim. Pablo Angeles David insisted on a policy of stamping out the Huks as a condition of accepting his appointment as governor of Pampanga. José Lingad, his successor in office and incidentally a former schoolmate of Taruc, continued this mailed-fist program.[5] Government troops, poorly trained, underpaid, and hard pressed, were sent out to eradicate the Huk menace. Barrios shielding Huk units were shelled. In a desperate effort to secure information the troops were sometimes guilty of maltreating suspects in an attempt to make them talk. This indiscriminate terrorism turned the people against the government and strengthened the Huk movement.

The Huks posed as protectors of the people. They collected taxes and a share of the rice harvest. They liquidated, that is, murdered government officials and agents—sometimes in broad daylight. Huk bands of 100 to 1,000 moved from place to place through Central Luzon. In encounters the government troops were often outnumbered.[6] The Philippine Army estimated that at the height of their power the Huks had 100,000 members with as many as 12,000 armed, active soldiers in the field. In numbers, organization, and small arms the Huk fighting units were comparable to the government forces. In terms of morale and civilian support in the area of their operations they had a decided advantage.

When the policy of all-out force brought no quick results, the government turned to a policy of mediation. A three-months truce was arranged, during which teams of government and Huk representatives were supposed to travel together from barrio to barrio to persuade the dissidents to lay down their arms and return to a peaceful life. But the terms of the truce

were never carried out. Huk representatives harangued crowds
of people with Communist propaganda. Government representatives were often heckled by unsympathetic listeners in the
barrios. During this truce one of the Huk leaders, Juan Feleo,
while under the "protection" of government agents, disappeared. The Communists claimed that he was kidnapped and
murdered. The truce ended in bitter fighting.

Throughout the term of office of President Roxas and until
his death in 1948 efforts were made by several government officials to bring about peace through a general amnesty for all
forces, but the president himself was never willing to make the
compromises necessary to secure Huk acceptance. A minority
coalition of leaders both in and out of Congress carried on correspondence with Roxas in an effort to find a basis for negotiat-
ing an amnesty.[7] Among them were Carlos Garcia, Judge Jesus
C. Barrera, and Antonio Araneta, all now high officials in the
Magsaysay administration.

Ignoring their efforts at mediation, Roxas intensified the conflict by urging the government forces to renewed action. In
March 1948, only a month before his death, he declared the
Huks and their supporting organization, the PKM,[8] illegal
and seditious:

"After careful and thorough deliberation and upon the recommendation of the Secretary of the Interior, the Secretary of
Justice, the Secretary of National Defense, the Chief of Constabulary and the governors of the provinces of Central and
Southern Luzon now being harassed by lawless elements, I
have today declared the Hukbalahap, headed by Luis Taruc,
and the Pambansang Kaisahan Manggagawa (PKM), headed
by Mateo del Castillo, as illegal associations organized and
maintained to commit acts of sedition and other crimes, for the
purpose of overthrowing our present government under the
Constitution by wresting the reins of government from the law-
fully-elected representatives of the people and establishing a
government of their own, through force and intimidation.

"The Hukbalahap and the PKM are allied and complemen-
tary associations. Although the former is directly charged with
the undertaking of military operations, and the latter with the
political, economic and propaganda activities, they act jointly

and in close collaboration.'"[9] At the time of the death of President Roxas the opposing forces were sharply divided.

The new administration of Elpidio Quirino reversed the stern military policy of his predecessor and attempted to bring the Huks into the government's fold through conciliation and sweet reasonableness. Through the offices of the *Manila Chronicle,* contacts were made with the Huk leaders in the field. Negotiations carried on by Luis Taruc and the president's brother, Antonio Quirino, stretched over several weeks.[10] The Communist party debated what to do. The president's proposed amnesty had taken the political initiative out of their hands. Finally, with one dissenting vote, the party leaders decided to allow Taruc to proceed to Manila,[11] where he was received by the president and royally entertained. Taruc was given the seat in Congress which had been denied to him at the end of the election in 1946 on the grounds that force and terrorism had been employed during the balloting in Central Luzon.[12] But under the conditions of the amnesty all of this was to be forgiven and forgotten.

What each side expected from the amnesty is not entirely clear, but without question the government believed this would end hostilities. They prepared to receive the dissidents and their arms. The Huks were more wily in their expectations. They demanded extensive reforms in government and in the economy generally. Until these reforms were carried out they refused to disarm. But as the president pointed out, the reform program would take years. As weeks passed, charges of bad faith were hurled by both sides. Only a few Huks had registered and only a token number of arms had been surrendered. Having collected his back pay as a congressman, Taruc disappeared into Huklandia;* and the fighting began once more. The government's mailed fist had failed, and now the contrary policy of the kid glove had also proved inadequate.

The year 1949 was an election year, and it nearly led to disaster! Quirino and the Liberal party were opposed by wartime President José Laurel and the Nacionalistas. It was a bitter, close race. Quirino boasted of his friendly relations with Uncle

* Huklandia is composed of the four provinces, Pampanga, Nueva Ecija, Tarlac, and Bulacan.

Sam. But the Liberal party administration, which had failed to settle the Huk problem or to clean out graft and corruption in government, was losing ground. Laurel tried desperately to shake the stigma of collaboration. His supporters took the view that his great experience and strong leadership were needed for the present crisis. In an election marked by high temper and much violence, Quirino won by a narrow margin; yet he won under circumstances which lost him the confidence of the people: votes were bought, voters were terrorized, ballot boxes were stuffed or stolen, returns were padded. In some places more ballots were cast than the total of the population: the names of children, of dead persons, and of birds and flowers padded the voters' lists. People throughout the islands began to despair of democracy. In the dark days which followed, many turned hopeful eyes to the Huks and either actively joined their ranks or regarded them with sympathy.

Uncritical citizens were impressed with the strength of the Huk organization. There were extensive areas in the provincial hinterlands that were considered Huk territory. In these places the Huks constituted the final source of authority. They made and enforced laws, collected taxes, and organized the life of the people in support of the revolution. Even in the areas where the government troops patrolled during the day, the Huks took charge after dark. It became an axiom of the struggle that whichever side controlled peace and order after dark controlled the loyalty of the people.

The Huks had an elaborate educational system. Short-term schools were established for illiterates. At a higher level young people were introduced to Communist ideas and tactics. The following list will give some idea of the extent of this program.[13]

CURRICULUM FOR HUK SCHOOLS

Schools and Subjects	Number of Teaching Days
Primary schools	
Resolutions of Central Committee conferences . . .	7
Communist party	4
HMB: recruitment and organization of the liberation movement	4
Intelligence network	3

CURRICULUM FOR HUK SCHOOLS (*Cont.*)

Schools and Subjects	*Number of Teaching Days*
Intermediate schools	
History of the association	7
Present economic system	7
Present state of the government	7
History of peasant and labor movement	7
PKP—vanguard of liberation movement	7
Role played by HMB in the armed struggle	7
New democracy	7
Resolution of the Central Committee	7
Bookkeeping and accounting	3
High schools	
Dialectical materialism	10
Political economy	10
The imperialist	10
The state and revolution	10
Importance of the PKP	5
Political strategy and tactics	10
Military strategy and tactics	5
New democracy	5
Proletarian morals	5
Principles and techniques of teaching	10
New documents	10
Curriculum for the advanced school	
Dialectical materialism	7
National problem	7
Agrarian problem	7
HMB to regular army	7
New democracy	7
Proletarian morals	7
Women problems	7
Evading tactics	7

Every bit of teaching material was either produced by the Communist party or was approved by the National Education Department of the party. To assist in this work of propaganda and education was the assignment of William Pomeroy, American Communist, who was an active member of the Huks until his capture in 1952.

In hidden mountain valleys the Huks had established villages and headquarters. Pomeroy describes one of these centers and its busy revolutionary activity:[14]

"Here was centered the National Educational Department of the Communist Party, under Peregrino Taruc, brother of Huk Supremo Luis Taruc. Here was the headquarters of the Communist Party's Regional Committee No. 4, which embraced the region covered by the provinces of Laguna, Quezon, Batangas and Cavite. Half an hour's walking distance away, was the headquarters of Casto Alejandrino, head of the Party's Military Department. Also, in that camp, a large force of organizers and soldiers was assembling under Mariano Balgos, Number Three Filipino Communist, in preparation for the long expansion march south into the Bicol provinces. A Reco (Regional Committee) school was in progress and at night, on the still air, the students could be heard singing and declaiming in regular cultural programs. A mimeograph machine in the office building clicked away all day long and into the night, turning out leaflets, documents and newspapers. There was no shortage of supplies; a 'dugout' was stacked to the roof with paper, stencils and ink, and more kept arriving steadily from the towns, slung on the back of Huk soldiers in the burlap cargo sacks that were the most distinguishing feature in the mountains. It could be said in fact, that the ordinary Huk soldier literally carried the revolutionary movement on his back, uncomplainingly, in the worst of weather, over the worst of terrain.

"Couriers, mostly young girls and boys chosen for their inconspicuousness, came and went in a steady stream, from the city, from the Party District Committees and Section Committees in the provinces, from the Field Commands of the Huk Army. At times, they bore with them, in the woven *bayongs* [palm-leaf sacks] of the ordinary marketer, as much 'mail' as a letter carrier would haul about in the city. Each time the couriers or the soldiers went out, on missions or supply trips, it meant anywhere from one day to one week of walking each way, through steep and often treacherous mountain trails."

The nerve center of the movement was located in Manila. This was the "Politburo-in," or the Political Bureau operating in secret from the inside. It was this organization which was smashed in the October 1950 raids and in the follow-up raids by government agents the next year. The Huks never recovered from this loss. There was also a "Politburo-out," which directed the revolutionary activity in the field. After the loss of the Manila Center, the Politburo-out had to assume all responsibility. (See organizational chart in Appendix.)

The Huks divided the Philippines into ten Regional Commands, or RECOs, with top party leaders assigned to each. These were military divisions, each with its own system of supply and intelligence and having a number of squadrons of about one hundred men each. To every organizational unit was assigned at least one party member. Others were sympathizers but not necessarily Communists under party discipline.

Every party member belonged to a cell, or nucleus, of three to five members. The sense of discipline, the submission of the individual will to that of the group developed in the life of the cell. In cell meetings party members had to bare their own weaknesses in self-criticism; then they had to point out flaws in other cell members. The net effect of these experiences was to produce intensely loyal and self-abnegating individuals.[15]

Those members of the Huks who were not Communists also labored under a strict discipline, as in the treatment of deserters: "Those who surrender but do not betray the Huks will be caught and tried by court martial. If they are not guilty of betrayal, they will be sentenced to hard labor. If they refuse to rejoin the Huks and refuse to comply with orders, they will be killed. Any who betray the Huks will be killed immediately."[16]

Financial support for the revolutionary activities came from several sources. Large gifts came from a few Chinese supporters; some funds came from per capita tax levies in the areas under Huk control. Gifts of food and medical supplies were supplemented by outright confiscation of goods. Raids, holdups, train robberies brought in large sums. In 1952 the Huk leaders drew up a budget calling for a monthly expenditure of almost ten million pesos.[17] This level of financing was never attained by the party National Finance Committee, but the actual expenditures were nevertheless impressive. The Cash Account Book of Regional Command No. 2 for the month of July 1951 shows expenses of ₱10,047.25 and cash on hand, ₱5,100.[18]

Impressed by their own strength and encouraged by the failures of government, the Huks decided that the time had come, with the 1949 elections, to make a bid for control of the Philippines.[19] They staged raids in 1949 and 1950 on an increasingly larger scale; there were plans of climaxing these with a final victory in 1951. Faced with these attacks, the Constabulary, which had been remarkably ineffective in Central Luzon, made the mistake of killing innocent civilians in a fight at Maliwalu, Pampanga. Another seventeen civilians were killed in Tarlac. Cries of "outrage" arose from every quarter. Civilians said that they preferred to live with the Huks rather than with the Constabulary. An army major even admitted in a public journal, "The increase in the number of dissident elements and their sympathizers in Central Luzon during the past few years may largely be attributed to the misconduct of officers and men who have been entrusted with the enforcement of law and order."[20]

The administration was forced to act to save itself. President Quirino went on a speaking tour to Constabulary posts and threatened swift court-martial to erring soldiers. He urged troops to inspire confidence and a sense of security among the civilians. In the *Philippines Herald,* on June 15, 1950, the president said that he wanted no repetition of the incident at Maliwalu, Pampanga. Referring to these sordid events, a Philippine army officer wrote, in an unpublished manuscript, "Even the Army is convinced that not all the Huks are really sympathizers of Taruc, but have only joined them because they or somebody among their kin has been abused by the soldiers."

In 1950 the Philippine government had failed to solve the Huk problem, but through all these failures had come understanding. The government had learned that it must meet force with force. This meant a drastic reorganization of the armed forces in order to gain supremacy on the battlefield. The government had also learned that it could not fight the Huks effectively unless it won the respect and co-operation of the civilians. This meant a new and different approach by the officers and soldiers. Finally, the government had learned that a policy of dealing justly and humanely with the Huks—the policy of attraction—could undercut the Huk appeal to the common people. This meant a program of psychological warfare, supported by effective reform measures designed to solve social problems. The stage was set for a new leader to wage an effective campaign against the forces of communism in the new republic. Needed, a leader! Enter Ramon Magsaysay!

This new Secretary of the Department of National Defense, appointed in September 1950, was a congressman from Zambales. Though not an experienced politician, this amateur was to show the way to a new kind of politics in the Philippines. He had fought the Japanese as a guerrilla leader during the war, and he had successfully operated a small transportation company. His motto had been, "When an engine breaks down, fix it." He carried this simple philosophy of action with him as he directed the nation's armed forces in their struggle with the Huks.

He did more; he lived his own philosophy of action. When the troops campaigned, Magsaysay was there. When a soldier was killed in action, Magsaysay was there to express his care and concern. When acts of bravery were performed, Magsaysay was there to command and promote the officers and men. When the troops were in need, Magsaysay was there with supplies, increased appropriations, and logistical support. And when the Huks surrendered or were captured, Magsaysay was there to listen to their stories and to see that they received fair treatment. This man with boundless energy and a heart responsive to human need rallied the nation. His men worked around the clock and slept only when they were exhausted. The country took courage: democracy was on the march!

The first move was the reorganization of the armed forces, integrating the Constabulary with the army and creating a unified command under the Chief of Staff. General Duque was promoted to this position and began at once in January 1951 to attack the problem of army morale. Undesirable officers and men were discharged or retired; effective officers were promoted. Salaries and allowances were increased. Performance in the field received special recognition. Abuse of civilians was severely punished. For example, military intelligence agents who manhandled a newsman and a bookstore operator were faced with immediate court-martial.[21] Newly appointed civil-affairs officers joined service clubs and participated in community activities. They undertook the important tasks of interpreting the army to the people and of winning civilian support for the army activities against the Huks. Gradually the hostility to the fighting forces changed to respect and gratitude. A new campaign to collect unregistered firearms met with great success. Magsaysay said in a radio address, "I felt that before we could meet the peace and order problem in earnest, it was necessary first to restore the confidence of our people in their armed forces."

Not content to pursue Huks and kill Huks, Magsaysay wished to win them back to the government's side through a positive program of social reform. Establishing a practice of talking to anyone who came to his office, and of holding interviews with captured and surrendered Huks, he educated himself to the people's needs and sharpened his sensitive spirit to the basic problems of those on the other side in Huklandia. He learned that the strong popular support of the Huks among the peasants of Central Luzon was rooted in real agrarian problems. Why not inaugurate some generous and dramatic program to meet the needs of the peasants? The Communists had promised "land for the landless." The government had unoccupied public lands; why not give land to the landless? Colonies of settlers had been established in Mindanao before the war,[22] but the postwar efforts had been stalled by bureaucratic red tape and corruption. General Duque and other officers had once planned a homestead settlement for retired army men, but the plan had been shelved for lack of funds and top-level support.

Magsaysay now revived the idea of the settlement primarily as a project for landless Huks. A small percentage of ex-army men could be included as a stabilizer group. The army could provide security for the settlers and aid them in planting their first crops. A grubstake could be arranged until the settlers were self-supporting. Thus the plans took shape. In one dramatic move the army would undercut the Huk propaganda and appeal to the peasants. At the same time it would rehabilitate ex-Huks and offer a strong inducement for others to surrender.

Magsaysay put the plan into effect. The Army Appropriations Act for 1951 provided for the organization of ten additional Battalion Combat Teams, and authorized that "any balance from said appropriation may be used to defray expenses for the rehabilitation of captured or surrendered dissidents."[23] The secretary managed to save enough pesos from this budget to establish the Economic Development Corps (EDCOR) as a part of the army.[24] Soon a group of EDCOR engineers left for Mindanao to survey the site for the first settlement and to begin clearing land and building roads. Their enthusiasm was fired with the thought that in this campaign they were building for peace and not for destruction.

The EDCOR Farms created a radically new role for the army. No longer were the armed forces limited to defending the nation and destroying the enemy. The army was to serve the people in a new way—constructively and creatively. It would rehabilitate the Huks and restore them to the nation as loyal, productive citizens.

A foreign news correspondent months later looked in amazement upon this new settlement. Soldiers were erecting poles and stringing electric lines to settlers' homes. Ex-Huks with bolos swinging at their sides were discussing their farm problems with unarmed settlement officers. The newsman said, "I have seen many armies, but this one beats them all. This is an army with a social conscience." The Philippine Army had not always acted with "conscience," but through the painful experience of civil war it had learned that only that force which meets the needs of the people can redeem the nation.

The EDCOR settlements were to demonstrate a new concern of government for the people, a concern which was to find expression in a program of village improvement, attention to school needs, the drilling of wells in places where safe drinking water was a problem, the increase in efficiency in government bureaus, the insistence upon clean elections, and honesty in political office. EDCOR was a foretaste of a new diet in Philippine democracy.

CHAPTER THREE

THE LAND OF PROMISE

South of Manila five hundred miles lies the island of Mindanao, second largest in the Philippines and one of the most fabulous frontiers of the world today. Its population is varied, including the colorful Moros of Lanao Province, the pagan tribes of Bukidnon and the remote mountainous areas, and the rapidly increasing Christian Filipino communities in the coastal plains and the newly settled areas of Zamboanga, Cotabato, Davao, and Agusan. Mineral deposits and natural resources have only begun to be developed. A power plant recently was opened on the north coast at Maria Christina Falls. At present this power is used to manufacture fertilizer, but a steel mill is to be added in the future. Coal is mined in southern Zamboanga, iron ore in Surigao, gold in Davao. Uranium deposits have been located in the mountains near Davao City. Thousands of acres of forests containing some of the finest hard woods in the world cover the mountain slopes and valleys.[1] The soil is so fertile that farmers must use a cover crop to prevent the weeds and young trees from taking over between harvest and planting. Here in this land of promise the EDCOR began its first settlement early in 1951.

Spurred by the eagerness of the Secretary of Defense, a handful of newly appointed EDCOR officers and men enplaned for Ozamis City, the nearest airport to the contemplated farmsite in Lanao Province. From this point they took a launch across the bay to the eastern shore, where they were met by army jeeps and carried to the end of the road to Kapatagan. From here the party proceeded on foot several miles to the barrio of Buriason, which at that time was little more than a name. The surveyors had already crossed several rivers; now they camped on the bank of another. The jungle crowded in close about them. Giant trees disappeared in a tangle of green foliage overhead. Trails visible for only a few feet ahead led off through the forest. Monkeys "churrumped" in protest against the invasion of their preserves. Brilliantly plumed wild fowl cut streaks of color through the underbrush. The noise of heavy objects crashing through brush signaled the presence of wild hogs. In these haunts had lived a Moro outlaw named Datu Tawantawan. His surrender and the quitclaims of other Moros who had long lived in the area paved the way for the government to settle in that place.[2]

The survey party crisscrossed the valley. The land was nearly flat in the center and sloped gently toward the mountains that rose sharply to the south and east. Mount Iniaon cast a long shadow across the valley as it held back the first rays of the early morning sun. Water was abundant in streams and springs. A pipe driven a few yards into the earth would produce an acceptable well. The townsite was laid out on this plain near the mountains, a beautiful setting for a new community.

Under the leadership of Colonel Ciriaco Mirasol the men went to work. Clearing land with hand tools was backbreaking toil. Tractors and bulldozers and power saws were to come later, but for the present this pioneer army unit had little to go on except the order to begin and the faith and energy of Mirasol.

Civilian settlers within ten miles of the site were invited to help in the clearing. At first they were slow to respond, but they soon appreciated what the presence of the army unit and the new settlement would mean to them in terms of protection, medical care, schools, roads, and markets. They began to lend their efforts to the project, bringing with them their own axes and their own lunches. These were free contributions of labor, since at the beginning Mirasol did not have a centavo of money to spend on the project. But as the work progressed, men, equipment, and funds were sent from the army headquarters at Camp Murphy near Manila. Civilians were then employed to build houses for the settlement. Bulldozers started scraping a road to the new project. Dead tired at night, the men would crawl into their tents and try to sleep. To the noises of the jungle were added the weird sounds of the *kolintong,* a set of gongs which is the favorite musical instrument of the Moros. In this environment the army's experiment in land settlement began.

Everything was done in a hurry during these early months. The EDCOR field teams started their work in February; barely three months later the first group of twenty-six settler families arrived. Although the buildings and roads were far from completed, Captain Jongko, who had been appointed

Farm Administrator under the over-all direction of Colonel Mirasol, was able to provide the settlers with houses and a hall for meetings.

Additional groups of settlers came in June and in August. Each family was given a house on a town lot approximately sixty by one hundred feet in size. Their first task was to fence the yard and to plant a garden. This took one to two months; then the settlers were ready to begin work on their farms.

At this point the first major problem arose. In the rush of other activity, the survey of farm lots had not been completed. The settlers began to grumble, "We might as well go home if we are not going to have a farm." A tentative assignment of lots turned out unhappily, because many of the settlers had to be reassigned to different lots when the final survey was finished.[3] But these were growing pains produced by the rapid pace of the development. On the positive side, the administration could boast of completed houses for the settlers, a school for children through the sixth grade, an administration building and quarters for the army officers and men, roads graded and surfaced, electric lights in all buildings and houses, and a medical service and dispensary. An American visitor during these early days said, "I don't believe that in the trail-blazing days in my own country two hundred years ago our pioneers could have done a better job of transformation for the brief period of only four months."[4]

The total area covered by the EDCOR project at Kapatagan is 1,680 hectares,* or about 4,000 acres. Subtracting the area devoted to the townsite and some 68 claims by Christian Filipinos and another 11 by Moros, which were recognized as legitimate prewar homestead claims, there were 126 farm lots, 6 to 10 hectares in size, for distribution to EDCOR settlers. A few of these near the townsite were reserved for possible town expansion. Approximately 100 EDCOR settlers could therefore be accommodated.[5] This would make a good small community, but it was not large enough to meet the needs of the ex-Huks. Another EDCOR farm was therefore opened in the adjacent Province of Cotabato in November 1951.

The new project at Buldon is an hour's rough drive by jeep north of Cotabato City. Here, at an elevation of some 1,500 feet,

* One hectare is equal to 2.471 acres.

army surveyors found a suitable site for a new settlement on public lands that had been set aside by the government a number of years before. The land lies at the base of sharp-peaked mountains in the rolling foothills, where the Simuay River cuts through in its rush toward the sea. The farmlands, though rough and hilly, proved excellent for growing coffee, upland rice, bananas, ramie, and vegetables. Mornings in this higher altitude are clear and brisk; afternoons are almost always cloudy and rainy. The nights are cold enough to require a wool blanket for comfortable sleeping.

The first project at Kapatagan, in contrast to the new one at Buldon, is located on flat and marshy land where the climate is hot and humid. Rains continue throughout the year, but are lighter and less frequent during the "dry" season. The differences in terrain and climate dictate different types of agriculture.

The townsite at the Buldon EDCOR Farm is located across the river from the farm lots on flat land that had been part of the ancestral holdings of two Moro brothers, Royod and Maluag Sandab. They had filed a claim in Cotabato for this land but, like most other land claims in Mindanao, the patent had not yet been granted. Through requests by officials and army officers, the Moros were persuaded to donate first 60 and then an additional 24 hectares of land to EDCOR for use as a townsite. The terms of the gift, first made in an oral agreement between the Sandabs and Farm Administrator Alcantara, specified a strip 300 meters wide and 2 kilometers long on the west bank of the Simuay River. When the agreement was put in writing, however, only total area was specified, and no mention was made of the shape of the donated plot. Here lay the makings of difficulty and misunderstanding.

Army engineer P. S. Torio, in charge of laying out the town, was a dashing, energetic, efficiency-conscious major after the leadership pattern set by Mirasol and Jongko. When he laid out the town, he made no effort to confine it to a 300-meter strip along the river. Following the original strip agreement, several individuals had already bought land adjacent to the proposed town and the projected highway. Torio's plan would cut through their claims. Brushing aside their objections, he ordered the individuals to move back. They moved, but not far

enough to suit the engineer. One irate claimant chased a bull-
dozer operator off "his land" with a bolo. In defending his action the major explained, "We had to build a town, not a landing strip. The signed agreement permits us to locate on any
sixty hectares within the claimed holdings of the Moro Datus."[6]
Colonel Alcantara, a flexible and kindly administrator, coun-
seled peace and forbearance. The argument over the western
boundary dragged on for weeks, but in the end was amicably
settled. In the meantime the community rapidly developed according to the pattern of wide streets carved in the earth by
Torio's bulldozers. The wide and spacious plan amply justified the engineer's stubborn effort.

In addition to the rows of neatly thatched cottages, an impressive civic center was developed. When the settlers cele-
brated the first anniversary of the founding of their community, they could boast a complete elementary school and a large
cleared playground, a hospital and clinic, a tennis court, a
church, a reading center and officers' club, a partly completed
building where town meetings were held, an administration
building, a motor pool and storage building, and a plant nursery and piggery. A communications building housed a radio
unit and a power plant which delivered electric current to the
home of every settler. A spring was improved and diverted into
a covered reservoir from which water was piped to convenient
faucets throughout the community. Periodic tests ensured that
the water was safe to drink. The engineers built a heavy log
bridge across the Simuay River, connecting the townsite with
the farm lots. A central farm road and a main lateral road were
cleared with bulldozers.[7] Perhaps this list may not impress an
urbanized Westerner, but in the rural Philippines it sounds
like an H. G. Wells account of things to come.

As in Kapatagan, the most thorny problem of the early days
of the settlement arose over the distribution of the farm lots.
The first survey, in which the area was plotted into 255 farms,
was made from maps, with little attention paid to actual con-
tours. One of the lots went almost straight up a steep cliff; another was located astride a fork in the river. In an area that is
rugged and crossed by a swift, wide river, a good field survey
was an absolute necessity. While the resurvey progressed
slowly, the settlers became restless and began to grumble. Colo-

nel Mirasol was constantly called in to listen to complaints. In July 1952 the settlers staged a demonstration against the officers at the farm. In October, when army officers are normally rotated, Major V. O. Valenova became the new Farm Administrator. At the time he assumed his responsibilities there were still many settlers without an assignment of a farm lot. With great skill and patience this soldier, who had worked with General Santos on land settlement projects in Mindanao during the prewar period[8] and who had fought the Japanese in the invasion at near-by Parang Bay, began to sort out the problems and make progress toward solving them. Soon all the settlers had farms and were busy clearing the land and preparing for the first planting.

When the army created the Economic Development Corps, it initiated a program for which its officers had little specific training. The nature of the problems called for knowledge of agriculture, but the essential task of rehabilitating ex-Huks required some familiarity with social and psychological processes. Some of the officers were trained engineers; others were graduated from the agricultural branch of the University of the Philippines at Los Baños. None was trained in the social sciences. Their efforts and successes in the field of human relations were those of amateurs devoted to their tasks and willing to learn through experience.

The settlers were recruited chiefly from among the ex-Huks and suspects in the army stockades. Anyone without criminal charges against him was eligible to apply for a place in EDCOR. All settlers were volunteers; only those who indicated a willingness to go were taken. Applicants filled out a one-page questionnaire as to former employment, schooling, age, marriage status, and dependents. The EDCOR Administration did not record whether a prospect was a Communist party member, or what part he had taken in the Huk movement. The emphasis was placed on creating a community in which the past could be forgotten. The applications were passed upon by area commanders of the Armed Forces of the Philippines, or by the General Headquarters at Camp Murphy. In some instances applicants for the settlements were approved directly by the Secretary of National Defense. The

EDCOR farms accommodated every eligible ex-Huk and suspect who applied.

At both settlements now there is a stabilizer group composed of ex-soldiers, ex-guerrillas, and civilians, who receive the same privileges as the other settlers and who are chosen to leaven the community with loyalty and good citizenship. This group was selected with great care from among several thousand applicants. The prospect must have been a farmer but without land of his own, a Filipino citizen at least twenty-one years of age, married, physically able to do heavy farm work, loyal to democratic principles, and eager to co-operate in making a good community. He must be interviewed by the chief of EDCOR, or his representative, and must bring with him to this interview a certificate of good health from an army or government physician. He also must bring a clearance from the Philippine Constabulary, the local police agency, the mayor of his municipality, the justice of the peace, or the Military Information Service. If this interview is successful, the chief of EDCOR recommends that the applicant be accepted. This recommendation is forwarded to the Chief of Staff, who in turn sends it to the Defense Secretary, where final approval or rejection is made.[9] The successful applicant, feeling by this time that he must be a very important person, joins the next group going to Mindanao. There he lives alongside ex-Huks and tries to show what it means to be a good farmer and a good neighbor.

All settlers, both ex-Huks and civilians, sign a contract with the Armed Forces of the Philippines. The army promises to help in the initial clearing and cultivation of part of the land, to provide a house on the residential lot, and to sell on a credit basis the necessary work animals, tools, and food needed in developing the farm. Accounts are kept for each settler. He is charged for the actual cost of his house: ₱306.30* if the walls are of nipa material, and ₱358.90 if the walls are of wood. When he is issued tools, a carabao, and other equipment, these also go on his account. He is eligible for regular issues of rice and other foods to feed himself and his family until he harvests a crop and becomes self-supporting. A single man with no dependents eligible for a food allowance of ₱1.20 a day; a hus-

* Two pesos equals one dollar.

band and wife may draw up to ₱2.00 a day in the form of food; a husband and wife and four or more dependents may draw the maximum of ₱3.50. All of this is added to their account. When the settler begins to harvest his crops, he may start paying off his debts to the government. No more than 50 per cent of his harvest may be taken to reduce the sums that have been advanced to him. In actual practice, an amount of palay (unhusked rice) is set aside which will be sufficient for the family's food until the next harvest and for seed for the next planting. Whatever surplus is left can then be used in paying the account. This arrangement amounts to a noninterest-bearing loan to the settler until he can become self-supporting.[10]

The settler promises in the contract to live on his land at the EDCOR farm with no more than thirty days a year absence, to abide by the laws of the community, and to develop his farm in a manner satisfactory to the EDCOR administration. He promises that he will perform the work of the farm himself and not become a party to a system of tenancy. The army promises to assist settlers in securing titles to their land under the Public Land Act. If the title is granted before the loan is repaid, the loan becomes a mortgage against the property. In case a settler should die or become ill and unable to engage in farming before the terms of the contract are fulfilled, his heir or one of his relatives may take his place and enjoy the same rights and privileges, provided he also assumes any remaining obligations. Thus, the generosity of EDCOR is surrounded with realistic limits. Such services as transportation, farm supervision, protection, elementary schooling, water and lights, and medical care are free. The town lot and the farmlands are free. But in time the settlers will pay for everything else; this is their responsibility in a co-operative venture.

On April 21, 1953, three officers and two enlisted men from the Army Engineers were on their way to Isabela Province to inspect the progress in preparing the site for a third EDCOR farm. The plan which had worked successfully in Mindanao was to be tried on Luzon nearer the homes of the Huks. On the winding road through the mountain passes between the plain of Central Luzon and the Cagayan Valley the army jeep ran into a Huk ambush. All five men died in their seats in a burst of gunfire from the side of the road. This was the Communist answer to a constructive program.

When the opening day for the third project was set for January 18, 1954, the army decided to invite the people from the neighboring barrios in Isabela Province to join in the celebration. Since the farm was on the far side of the wide Cagayan River and miles from the thickly settled areas, the officers in charge of food and entertainment prepared for only two hundred guests. But they did not count on the fame of EDCOR and the curiosity of the people to see what the government was doing for ex-Huks. News of the opening spread rapidly through the countryside. Early in the morning of the appointed day the guests began to arrive. Men, women, children, and babies, they came on foot, on carabaos, by jeep, and by truck. From fifty miles away they came. The crowds jammed the riverbank waiting for opportunities to cross. All available boats and rafts were pressed into service. The only motor launch shuttled back and forth with loads of passengers so heavy that the boat developed a dangerous starboard list.

At the new EDCOR townsite the people milled around and curiously examined the neat modest wood houses, the running water, and the electric lights. They strolled back and forth along winding streets and gathered at the speakers' stand under a broiling sun for the opening ceremonies. A memorial plaque in honor of the ambushed army engineers was unveiled. The new project became Paredo EDCOR Farm, after Captain Roque A. Paredo. The older farms had already been rechristened: the one at Buldon became Gallego EDCOR Farm, in memory of Lieutenant Carlos A. Gallego, and the Kapatagan project became Arevalo EDCOR Farm, after Major Pablo V. Arevalo.[11] Thus a tragedy was turned into an honor to these men who were martyrs in a new phase of the struggle against communism.

After the speeches there was a wild scramble for the dining hall as more than two thousand people rushed to get a share of the food prepared for the expected two hundred. Brigadier General Balao, a tall six-footer and the honor guest of the occasion, stood head and shoulders above the others. He precariously balanced a plate of food above their heads while their elbows gouged into his sides. A Filipino in a broad-brimmed straw hat said jovially but not apologetically to an American visitor, "Push in and get something to eat; don't just stand there. This is our new democracy. No one is better than anyone else." No testimony could have been more eloquent praise of the Philippine achievement. The government had come to the people, and the people had responded with enthusiasm. EDCOR had become an important symbol of democracy.

CHAPTER FOUR

THE SETTLERS

Federico Baluyab was helping his father on a small, three-hectare rice farm in Pampanga when the war came to the Philippines.[1] They were tenants who struggled for a bare existence. According to customary practice, 50 per cent of each harvest went to the landlord. When the tenant's share was not enough to support the family, Baluyab borrowed from the landlord, who promptly at harvest time collected the loan, plus the customary 200 per cent interest. The family went deeper and deeper in debt. They never thought of government help, because in their eyes the government was run by the landlords.

Then the Japanese came. They were very demanding and severe. For failure to bow to the sentries near the town, Baluyab was made to sit in the sun for two days. When he asked for a pass to visit his relatives four kilometers down the road, he was slapped for being rude. Baluyab could never understand the Japanese, and he thoroughly resented the fact that they made life so unbearable. When his friend and cousin asked him to join the Hukbalahap guerrillas, he did so without hesitation.

That was 1943. At the end of the war in 1945, Baluyab, now Squadron Commander "Eagle," remained with the Huks. Things were not going well. Few of the Huk units were recognized by the American army; some of them were forcibly disarmed and the leaders placed in jail. Soldiers under the new Roxas government terrorized the people in the barrios where Huks had customarily stayed. Baluyab felt that the new government was even more oppressive than the Japanese. How could one be loyal to a government which offered "no redress for the killing of our people in the barrios?" The Huks, he thought, must be right in their objective of overthrowing the government and bringing about equality for all Filipinos.

Baluyab learned in 1947 that the Huk organization was Communist-led when he was assigned to the expansionist movement in Zambales. Up to this point he had worked without reservation for what he considered a patriotic cause; but when meetings were called to study Marxist theory and the

Communist "line," his enthusiasm began to cool. To fight for the rights of the poor was one thing; to bind oneself under Communist party discipline was something else. But Baluyab was too deeply involved in the movement to quit at this time.

A year later, in a fight between the army and the Huks, Baluyab's unit was separated from the larger force. He and twenty-five men started through the mountains to Tarlac. It was a frightfully long and arduous trip, begun with depleted energies and few supplies. Several of the men died of hunger and exhaustion on the way. In Tarlac the squadron had another encounter with the army, and Baluyab was wounded. He managed to reach Manila, where in time he recovered and then took party assignments around the city. One day a cousin talked to him and persuaded him to return to the hills. On their way an army patrol recognized them and began shooting. The cousin was killed, but Baluyab escaped.

Back in Manila a brother-in-law told Baluyab about EDCOR. "For the next few days, I kept thinking of a peaceful life and land of my own. I could not say no to it; I went to Camp Murphy and surrendered. To my surprise, the soldiers treated me well. I am convinced that this was a change made in the army by Magsaysay." Baluyab concluded, "More Huks would surrender if they knew about EDCOR."

EDCOR has many ex-Huks similar to Baluyab. They are men of conviction and idealism who joined the movement during the war, out of the double motives of hatred for the Japanese invaders and a sense of injustice at the hands of landlords. The transition after the war to an open, full-scale Communist revolt was not entirely to their liking. The subtleties of Communist theory were lost on this man, who had only a few years of schooling. Yet as long as he was an active revolutionary he made a wily and determined opponent.

Before he joined the Huks, Virgilio Panganiban was the Filipino equivalent of an American ward heeler, an amateur politician at the barrio level. During the rice-growing season, which lasts about half of each year, he worked as a tenant farmer on a five-hectare plot. After the harvest he combined the traveling vendor's trade with local politics.

During the 1946 campaign Panganiban worked hard for

President Osmeña and the Nacionalista ticket. As soon as the election was over, the victorious Liberals began to persecute their Nacionalista opponents. Panganiban, however, stood his ground for one more year. In the local elections for mayor in 1947 he was campaign manager for the Nacionalista candidate who lost. Fearing violence from the victorious party, he hid on his farm and avoided the town. But he was a marked man. The next year his harvest of 260 sacks of rice was confiscated by the civilian guards, an armed private police organization taking orders from the landlords and the leaders in the Liberal party. Convinced that political action against the party in power was useless, that he would not be allowed to farm peacefully, and that his life was in danger, he headed for the nearest headquarters of the Huks. Many of his friends had already joined. The Huks gave him a gun and offered to protect him against his enemies.

Panganiban is a natural leader. He is a large, strong man nearly six feet tall. His feet are broad and powerful from going barefooted and following a plow in the rice fields. He stands as straight as a mahogany tree in the forest. His eye is steady and betrays no embarrassment in the presence of "superiors." Although he has had no formal schooling, he speaks three different Filipino dialects fluently. The words tumble out clearly and forcefully. As commander of a Huk squadron he won the nickname "Black Terror."

One day in November 1950 the "Black Terror" and his men were on their way to a distant barrio when they met an army patrol. There was little protecting cover, but each side was determined to shoot it out. Panganiban was firing a .45 caliber pistol. While his arm was in the air from the recoil of the gun, a bullet struck him in the shoulder. The shot passed through the armpit and out the top side of his upper arm. Bleeding and helpless, he worked his way to a thicket and hid. The others dispersed, not knowing what had happened to their leader. Alone and feverish, next day he surrendered to the soldiers.

While in the army stockade Panganiban heard about EDCOR and volunteered to go. He was among the first settlers to arrive at Buldon and was elected the first mayor of the community. At present he is the proud father of a small son, an active member of the PTA, and a model settler. Communism had used this man, this rough diamond of humanity, but communism could lay no permanent claim to his allegiance when real opportunities were made available in a democratic community.

Sortero Valdes has a fiery temper and a sharp wit. As a youth of high-school age he joined a USAFFE* guerrilla unit in 1943 and was mustered out after the end of the war in 1946. He then completed his high-school course, got married, and began work in a small shoe factory.

Two years later his earnings were still low, prices were high, and he saw little prospect of anything better as a shoemaker. A friend talked to him about joining the Huks. Having little hope of a better job, he accepted the invitation. The Huks sent him to a branch of their Stalin University in the Sierra Madre Mountains of Laguna Province. Here he soaked up Communist doctrine under the instruction of William Pomeroy, an American ex-GI who had returned to the Philippines, married a Filipino girl, attended the University of the Philippines, and then become an important member of the Communist party leadership in the Huk.[2]

Valdes had joined the Huks because he believed in the program of helping the workers increase their earnings and of securing land for the peasants. After going to the Huk school and learning more about communism, he dreamed of a "new democracy" under the leadership of the proletariat, a democracy which would establish equality and free schools for everybody. He was told what was wrong with his country. Pomeroy taught him that all the ills in the Philippines came from a capitalist system that had been imposed upon the unsuspecting Filipinos by American imperialists. Having no intellectual resources to question these ideas, the youth accepted them as truth.

After this period of indoctrination Valdes returned to Manila to work under cover as a supply officer. One night in September 1951 he made his way cautiously between some stone monuments to a rendezvous spot in the Chinese cemetery. The "trusted" official he was to meet turned out to be a spy. He was surrounded by soldiers and army intelligence men who took

* United States Armed Forces in the Far East.

him prisoner. When Valdes was shown a file of evidence against him at Camp Murphy, he confessed to being a part of the Huk network in Manila.

"The army did not mistreat me," Valdes made a point to explain. "My confession was not forced from me under torture. After a few weeks, I was given an opportunity to come to EDCOR, and I consented to come. We had discussed EDCOR in the Manila Command before my capture. We thought it was just a trick to get us into a concentration camp; therefore we had decided not to surrender because of EDCOR." Later, when Valdes wrote his family in Manila about the good life at the Kapatagan EDCOR Farm, they would not believe him. His father and brother came all the way to Mindanao to prove to themselves that this was not just another army stockade.

Valdes is not entirely satisfied, however, with the arrangements at the EDCOR farm. He voiced some complaints: "We understood we would have free rations. We cannot repay all these charges against our accounts. The real ex-Huks here feel this way. We don't care what the other settlers think, but we Huks believe we are due free rations." Valdes is one of a small number of settlers whose orientation to the Communist doctrine is still strong enough to prevent full assimilation into the EDCOR community. This handful of men think of themselves as the "real ex-Huks" and in their own minds are separate from and superior to the other settlers. However, they are not troublemakers; their record on the farm is good. Two years is a short time to expect radical changes in the basic tenets of a man's beliefs. Given enough time, the free air of a healthy democracy may dissipate even the most stubborn Communist doctrine.

Manuel Padua is a handsome young idealist with a burning ambition to go to college and become a lawyer. While still a student in high school he became a member and later an organizer in the Democratic Peasants and Workers' Union in Iloilo Province on the island of Panay. The head of this union was José Nava, later convicted as a Communist on conspiracy and murder charges and sentenced to a life term in prison.[8] Frequent visitors from Luzon, such as Capadocia, del Castillo, and Paraiso, all well-known Communist leaders among the Huks, lectured to the union members. They also organized nuclei, small Communist cell groups of three to five members.

After the 1949 elections Capadocia came to Panay on a permanent assignment to expand the Huk organization and to lead the open rebellion against the government. One by one he picked his lieutenants and trained them in revolutionary tactics. While talking to Padua one day in a barrio near Iloilo, he said, "The legal struggle in the Philippines is no longer fruitful; you must join us in the hills and help us fight." In this way young Padua was drawn into the active Communist revolt.

His first assignment was to attend a course of lectures in the Huk school where Capadocia was the teacher. A program of reform was outlined. The Huks promised land to the landless, free primary education and free high schools,[4] jobs for the jobless, and free medical care and hospitalization, all of which appealed to the youthful idealism of Manuel Padua. Meanwhile his attractive personality and intellectual ability gained him recognition as a valuable leader. Capadocia commissioned him to head the expansion forces in the island of Negros, but when the work was little more than started he became ill and was captured.

Since there were no criminal charges lodged against Padua, he was eligible to come to EDCOR. He arrived with the first volunteers at Buldon, where he has become an industrious and exemplary settler. In appreciation for the new life he contributed an article, "Place of Rejuvenation," to the bulletin celebrating the first anniversary of the founding of the Buldon EDCOR Farm. Young Padua's association with the Huks had been broken before it had hardened into fanatical allegiance. Although he had played an important part in the affairs of the Communist party and in the Huk campaign on Panay and Negros, his idealism was never narrowly defined by Communist dogma. Possessing a keen and orderly mind and the flexibility of youth, he eagerly took advantage of the opportunities offered at EDCOR.

Some 63 per cent of the settlers at EDCOR are ex-Huks,[5] most of whose stories parallel the ones just narrated. Some, however, were on the fringe of the movement. They were carriers of supplies, or they belonged to the supporting peasant organization, the PKM.[6] The story of Artemio Morales shows

Mount Arayat and Candaba Swamp in Central Luzon provided
the Huks with hideouts not far from villages and towns.

The Huks raided and burned in the attempt to impress the people with their strength, 1948–50.

Can anything be salvaged from the ruins of this home which the Huks burned?

Homeless as a result of a Huk raid.

Defense Secretary Ramon Magsaysay (*left*) talked to William Pomeroy (*right*), American Communist among the Huks, after his capture in 1952.

Refugees from Huk terrorism sought protection in the public square of the city,

Settlers for the EDCOR farms in Mindanao were transported from Manila by the Philippine navy.

Abandoned by fleeing Huks, this infant was found almost dead, but has been restored to health by Lieutenant Peregrino in charge of the army nursery maintained for "Huklings."

The army clears the way for a farm road to a settlement for ex-Huks.

The first settlers arrive at Kapatagan EDCOR Farm.

The new EDCOR communities provide graded streets and inexpensive but comfortable houses.

Settlers inclosed their yards with fences, and planted gardens and fruit trees.

From the townsite at Kapatagan, the settlers have a scenic view of the mountains.

The army built a bridge across the Simuay River to link the townsite with the farm lots.

The strength of the EDCOR communities is seen in stable family life and the industry of the settlers.

Ex-Huk commander, capable and intelligent, finds that EDCOR provides real opportunities.

A woman, former Huk commander, said, "By working hard on my farm I can forget past suffering."

Youth and intellectual vigor once challenged by the Huk revolt now find a place of leadership in the town council at Buldon.

Ex-Huks at Isabela EDCOR Farm decorate their new home.

Ex-Huk and his family gather eggplant from a productive garden in their own yard.

Ex-Huks pit skill and brawn against the jungle.

The land is ready for planting, but far from "cleared."

Settlers build tiny houses on their farm lots where they can guard their crops from the monkeys and wild pigs.

Gigantic trees with flying buttresses made it necessary to build a scaffold where the woodcutter could work.

After the land is "cleared," the settler jabs holes in the dirt with a pointed stick and drops in the seed grain.

what happened to a man who had simply co-operated with the Huks.

Between 1946 and 1951 Morales was an overseer of a farm in an area where the Huks were frequent visitors. They came in armed bands and stopped and asked for food. Morales was hardly in a position to deny their request, since they were armed; moreover, their plea that they had no food and were hungry, while he had plenty, moved him to pity. "I felt merciful toward them and shared with them," he explained.

The Huks never asked Morales to join them, but he listened to their propaganda and especially liked the idea of equality. If the Huks won, they promised that there would be no rich and no poor. All the peasants would have land of their own.

Word reached the army that Morales was feeding the Huks. One morning while he was eating breakfast army men came in a truck and took him to the nearest detention center at Camp Ord. He pleaded that he was not a Huk, but his denial was unconvincing. The interrogators wrapped a cloth around his eyes and gave him a beating. After three months in the army stockade he volunteered to take his family to EDCOR, since he saw no possibility of returning to his former home.

After two harvests at the Kapatagan settlement Morales is able to support his family with no further government assistance. His eight-hectare farm is a model of industry and careful planning. With the help of relatives who have joined him on the farm and with an expenditure of about ₱1,000 which he had previously saved, he now has abaca and rice crops that may yield an income of as much as ₱12,000 a year. The family labor supply and private capital are not available to many of the settlers, but Morales had proved what can be done with the land. He points out that he still has no carabao and plow. His farm is a monument to hand labor.

Some 19 per cent of the settlers who had been classified as ex-Huks turned out upon investigation not to be ex-Huks at all. They had become involved in a net of circumstances and suspicion which got them into difficulty with the army, but they rightly should be considered only as "suspects." Two examples will give some idea about this group.

Simplicio Hilario joined the civil guard in 1947. This was

a landlord-sponsored organization to protect the plantations against the dissidents. Hilario was discharged in 1950. In answer to a letter from his father-in-law, he decided to accept an invitation to work on the family's farm in a barrio in Tarlac Province. Shortly after reaching his destination he was apprehended by a policeman and a plain-clothesman. Being a stranger in the community he was suspected of being a Huk and, more seriously, of participating in the bloody Makabulos Raid, a notorious Huk raid on Tarlac and on the Constabulary post on the outskirts of the town. Unfortunately, Hilario had left the letter from his father-in-law back in Nueva Ecija. The police would not free him to produce this evidence and explain his presence. Neither would they listen to his relatives who came to plead his innocence. They were taking no chance on letting a Huk suspect escape. Hilario was sent to the detention center at Camp Murphy, where he heard about EDCOR and volunteered to go to Mindanao.

Hilario claims that he had never seen a Huk or known one intimately enough to engage in conversation. This is probably an exaggerated statement in an attempt to establish his innocence. One could hardly have lived in the heart of Huklandia for years and have fought the Huks as a member of the civil guard without some intimate contact with the dissidents. Hilario is a drifter from job to job and place to place who was caught up in a web of suspicious circumstances. He manifests no firm loyalties either to the Huks or to the government. His record as a settler at EDCOR is mediocre. Instead of working hard and taking advantage of the opportunity to develop his own land as most of the other settlers have done, Hilario complains that he and his wife are all alone. While the season drags on, he waits for the government to provide money to transport his father to Mindanao to help on the farm. The government finds it as difficult to turn such drifters into self-supporting farmers as to convert ex-Huks into loyal citizens.

Felix Ocampo worked as a hauler of coconuts in San Pablo City, Laguna Province. One night when he returned home from work he was told that the soldiers wanted to see him. After dressing, he reported to the headquarters of the nearest

Battalion Combat Team. Secret agents questioned him and tried to force him to admit that he belonged to the Huks. But when repeated beatings produced no confession he was released.

Four days later his mother reported that the soldiers were again looking for Felix. Again he went to the army headquarters, where he was ordered to confess. This time, after a round of beatings the questioners used a form of punishment known as "sitting on air" in which Felix was forced to assume an awkward half-squatting position until he fell to the ground exhausted. After all this and still no confession, he was placed in the army stockade. Months later when he heard about EDCOR he volunteered to become a settler.

Behind the army's efforts to get the young Ocampo to talk were a long series of suspicious circumstances. It all began in an innocent attempt on the part of the Ocampos to befriend a wealthy neighbor family. The head of this household, a man thirty-eight years of age, was kidnaped by the Huks and held for ransom. His family in desperation asked the Ocampos to help make contact with the Huks, since Felix, in gathering coconuts from the outlying barrios, knew where the Huks passed. Felix and the brother of the kidnaped man went to a likely spot and waited. Soon an individual dressed like a soldier—but who turned out to be a Huk—came along the path. Engaging the pair in conversation, he explained his mission and demanded ₱12,000 in ransom. The money was paid to him directly, and soon the victim was released. But the suspicions circulated that young Felix knew too much about the Huks and their activities to be an innocent bystander. This was war, an evil civil war where friends and enemies were hard to distinguish. The writ of habeas corpus having been suspended in certain Huk-ridden provinces by presidential proclamation, only a shadow of suspicion was often enough to detain a man.[7] Thus Felix Ocampo became a Huk "suspect" and eventually a settler at EDCOR.

The stabilizer group, civilians composing 18 per cent of all the settlers, sets the pace on the EDCOR farms. To be sure, not all of them are star performers. A couple from Leyte, for example, were unhappy on the farm, and could think of nothing

good about it except that there are no typhoons in Mindanao.*
They complained bitterly that the administration had not
cleared their land, removed all the stumps and roots, and given
them a tractor so that they could be "modern" farmers. But
most of the stabilizers were more like an ex-sergeant at the
Kapatagan farm. With the assistance of his father he has
cleared and planted five hectares in abaca, the crop which is
the source of Manila hemp. The first plants are already mature
and ready for harvest. Once each quarter a new crop will be
ready for market. By conservative estimates the sergeant can
employ help in stripping out the fibers and still make ₱12,000
a year when his farm comes into full production. In addition,
he can easily grow most of his food on the remainder of his land.

Deep in the jungle across the river from the townsite at Buldon and far from the lateral farm road is a clearing, a small
hut, and a barking dog. This is the farm lot of Maria Florentino, once known among the Huks as Commander "Lusing."
She is one of five women ex-Huks or suspects who have become
EDCOR settlers. Although she is only thirty-seven years of
age, her hair is gray and her face shows the effects of much too
much suffering. Here in the wilderness, with only an occasional
visit to the town, she lives with a young boy who volunteered to
be her companion and helper.

At the time of the war Maria was married to an American
engineer and reserve army officer. When he joined the army
for active duty after Pearl Harbor, Maria parceled out her five
children among friends and volunteered as an ambulance
driver between Cavite and Bataan. She never saw her husband
again. Having organized an active guerrilla force to harass
the Japanese north of Bataan, he was caught during the early
days of the occupation and executed. Maria herself was intercepted by the Japanese advance north of Manila as she tried to
drive her ambulance back from Bataan for one last trip. Thinking that she possessed valuable military information, the Japanese tried to make her talk. Periods of solitary confinement
were interrupted by sessions of torture. She was beaten, then

* Leyte is in the typhoon belt and is subject to periodic and catastrophic dam-
age, while Mindanao is free of destructive winds.

made to kneel on broken bottles. Her finger nails were ripped off.

The Japanese tried a new tactic. In soft persuasive tones they said, "If you will work for us and help establish the new co-prosperity sphere in East Asia you will have an easy and comfortable life." Maria answered a curt "No!" Then the Japanese located three of her children, aged eight, nine, and ten, in a school in Manila and threatened to harm them if she did not co-operate. Her answer was still, "No." The children were lined up and bayoneted before her eyes, and the mother was sentenced to death. Just before the execution she was offered a job working in the Japanese hospital, and she accepted.

Every morning Maria was taken from the cell in Fort Santiago to the hospital; every afternoon she was returned. As days passed and she became a customary figure around the prison, the guards allowed her some freedom and had her prepare their coffee at night. Carefully she planned an escape. From the hospital she smuggled a pair of scissors and some sleeping pills. The pills went into the coffee. When both guards were sound asleep, she calmly stabbed them to death with the scissors and in company with seven other prisoners escaped.

For several months Maria hid in a small barrio in the mountains of Quezon Province. One night armed men came to the hut and took her away for investigation. Since she was a stranger in that place, they thought she might be a spy. She had become a prisoner of a Huk guerrilla unit. They gave her jobs around the camp but kept her under close surveillance for three months. Finally, convinced of her loyalty, the Huks took her to the headquarters of their section commander, who made her his office secretary. Later she was given a six-months indoctrination course in the Stalin University.

She graduated a confirmed Huk and was made a commander of a small squadron of twelve men. In one year she enlarged the unit to one hundred and sixty. It was an active unit. Commander "Lusing" was primarily interested in killing Japanese. The ambush and the quick raid were her favorite tactics.

During the liberation her squadron and the other units of the Banal Regiment were the only Huks officially recognized by the United States. After the fighting, she presented her men at Camp Murphy for mustering out. Some of them later returned to the mountains and to the Huks. Maria worked in the United States army hospital at Baguio and when it closed she came to reside in Manila. She tried to live quietly and unnoticed. When the Japanese were defeated, her incentive to fight ended. She had no heart for the postwar Huk revolt.

But one day near Quiapo Church in downtown Manila, Maria was recognized by one of her former soldiers. A jeep driven by a Huk pulled up to the curb, and Maria was asked to take a ride. The men were urgent: they needed her to come back and command her unit. It was a hard decision. She loved the peace after years of bloodshed, but how could she turn down the request of friends when they needed her? Besides this appeal to former friendship she also feared that the Huks might liquidate her if she refused. Thus Maria again became Commander "Lusing."

There followed three more years of guerrilla fighting. Then one day in February 1951, while her men were out on patrol, she was seated alone under a tree in the forest writing a report to Huk headquarters that she needed reinforcements in order to carry out the ambush they had ordered. Suddenly she was surrounded and captured by an army unit.

At the stockade, Filipino army men accused her of committing many crimes. When she denied these charges, she was slapped and beaten. On one occasion the questioners put her in a large ice box until she became unconscious. When she revived, she was covered with sand. The army agents gave her injections of something to break down her resistance. For a month after the ordeal she could not walk upright.

On the EDCOR farm in the depths of the jungle Maria Florentino has found peace and contentment. She is not a robust person; nevertheless, she does a hard day's work. Her production record equals that of most of the men settlers. She says, "I should like to forget the past. Perhaps after a few years when I am no longer able to farm I will have saved enough to open a small store."

Commander "Lusing," like others among her countrymen, was drawn into the Huk movement primarily because of bitterness toward the Japanese. Then wartime friendships and the hold of Communist teachings kept them active in the postwar movement. Maria understands Communist doctrine, and she is still sympathetic with the Huk reform program. But she is no doctrinaire Communist. Her loyalties go deeper than the party line. Because of her past suffering and her present brave effort, she has the admiration of every settler and soldier, man and woman, at Buldon.

These are the settlers at EDCOR. They come from thirty-four provinces and from Manila. Most of the settlers (61 per cent) are from Luzon; the next largest number (24 per cent) come from Panay. By provinces, the largest number come from Iloilo; Nueva Ecija ranks a close second; Leyte is a poor third, hard pressed by Pampanga and Pangasinan, which are tied for fourth.

The settlers range in education from illiterates to college graduates; however, there is only one college graduate among them, while 28 per cent have had no schooling. Some 60 per cent have a third-grade education or less. Only 15 per cent have had any high-school training. Though these figures indicate a community of low educational attainment, some of those with little formal schooling display remarkable ability and leadership.

A study of the occupational background of the ex-Huks before they joined the dissident movement shows that 69 per cent were engaged in farming. Of these, 46 per cent were tenants; another 44 per cent were helping their father, who was the tenant; 8 per cent were small landowners; and 2 per cent were squatters. The remainder of the ex-Huk settlers (31 per cent) come from varied occupational backgrounds: bus drivers, fishermen, shoemakers, watchmen, sign painters, sawmill workers, foremen, policemen, house servants, road workers, tailors, students; some of them were unemployed or only partly employed.

The settlers are mostly young men. Two years after EDCOR started, 10 per cent are still 21 years of age or younger. The average age is 32 years; only two settlers are over 60.

The average family size, including husband, wife, children, and other dependents, is now five. However, 20 per cent of the settlers had no dependents at the time they came to Mindanao. Small families of three or less were characteristic of 44 per cent of the cases.

Four out of every ten who came to live in the EDCOR farms

at Kapatagan and Buldon were unmarried. How to govern these young bucks in a wilderness where marriageable women were as scarce as paved roads became a major problem to the farm administration.

Here they were, the old and the young, the Huks and the suspects, the civilians and the soldiers, the educated and the illiterate, the married and the unmarried. Could purpose temper such diversity? If democracy succeeded here, its prophets could indeed take courage.

CHAPTER FIVE

WRESTLING WITH THE JUNGLE

Most of the settlers came from the flat lands of Central Luzon or from the coastal plain of Panay. Forests had been cleared from these areas for several hundred years. A folk culture of forest skills had long since disappeared from the lowlands, where generation after generation of farmers had only to plow and plant and harvest the neat, level rice paddies. The rice harvest was usually followed by a long vacation during which man and beast and land "lay fallow" until the next rainy season. Such farming customs provided a meager existence in the old provinces; in the virgin land of Mindanao they were wholly inadequate. Most of the settlers were ill prepared for the tests that lay ahead.

The EDCOR farms were surveyed and corners marked with a cement monument. Then the farms were distributed by lottery in which each settler drew a number from a hat. By matching his number with one on the large map of the surveyed area in the administration building he got some idea where his farm would be. With soldiers and administrators as guides, the settlers set out to find their land.

When the lowlanders first came face to face with the jungle, they were stunned. Instead of open fields that could be plowed, they found themselves staring at a tangle of green underbrush and vines that could only be penetrated by hacking a path with a bolo. Trees both large and small covered the land, and every fifty steps or so stood a giant of huge dimensions. Thick flying buttresses rose from the ground some fifteen feet high and tapered toward the main trunk, itself some twelve feet thick. Flying buttresses and trunks together spread over an area of twenty feet. These giants rose straight toward the heavens so high that one could not see the birds playing in the upper branches. Such a tree could not be cut near the ground because of the buttresses; the woodsman first had to build a scaffold. From this perch fifteen feet in the air he laboriously chipped away at the trunk. The trees were beautiful hardwoods, but the man chopping away with a small axe wasted little sentiment on their grandeur. After days of backbreaking labor down came the mountain of cellulose with a crash that shook the earth. Then came endless hours of lopping off the branches and burning the smaller limbs. But this was all that a man could do. The heavy unburned log lay across his land immovable by man or beast until years hence the white ants and rot returned it to earth.

Many of the settlers, when they saw these trees for the first time, sat down and wept. How could a man with an ax and a bolo make any impression on these forests? Their discouragement led to fear and despair. Some just sat at home or puttered in the garden. It took all the persuading, cajoling, and threatening of the farm administration to get them to return to their land a second time and begin clearing.

The EDCOR soon found it wise to help the settlers meet this initial problem. Sums of ₱60 per hectare for two hectares a year were made available to any settler unable to clear his own land. This amount was sufficient to employ the labor necessary to do the roughest work of cutting down the trees and underbrush. The money spent in this way was added to the settler's account, to be repaid later as his farm came into production.

During the months of September and November, 1953, the author interviewed a random sample of one-half the ex-Huks and suspects at Kapatagan and Buldon. Each settler was asked, among other questions, to discuss his problems and to express any complaints he had with life at EDCOR. Some 31 per cent of them either considered their existence blissful and problem-free, or were too shy to mention complaints. The other 69 per cent listed many problems, varying from the inroads of wild monkeys on their rice crops to the difficulties of finding a wife. Their problems as reported by the settlers themselves form a major part of this chapter.

Two years after the first settlers arrived at Kapatagan, and shortly after the first harvest at Buldon, problems of clearing the jungle and turning it into farmland were still paramount in the minds of the settlers. Their fight against the government had been transformed into a struggle with the jungle. In discussing their troubles, settlers most often mentioned the need for heavy bulldozers to clear the land. Even after the trees were felled, stumps and logs cluttered the land. Roots made plowing difficult or impossible. Some of the few settlers who had cara-baos and plows found they could not use them. The wife of one of the leading settlers said, "We are very discouraged because we have not received the help in the form of heavy equipment that was promised. As a result we must farm with primitive tools and methods. Our carabao is useless because of the roots, and we are told that it will be four years before they rot. In the meantime we are running up debts, already about ₱2,000. How can we ever pay this back?"

If they were left to clear the land by hand alone, many of the settlers believed the odds against them were too great. An ex-Huk said, "I cannot use my carabao and plow, and I cannot support my family by hand farming alone. I need help." The Old World picture of "the man with the hoe" would look good to many of these jungle pioneers. "At least, he is working cleared land," would be their comment. Another ex-Huk said, "Our problem now is to clean the land of stumps and logs. But if I am working only with my hands, I will be bleached bones here."

The answer to this problem of clearing the land is not easy. The EDCOR administration has had bulldozers for road building, but not the powerful heavy ones that would be needed in clearing large stumps and logs. The cost of such equipment is beyond the means of the settlers. The EDCOR budgets are already pressed to the limit. Is this a cost which the government should undertake? Are there no other alternatives to mecha-nized land clearing? Some of the settlers themselves have found one answer. They leave the timber where it falls and burn what-ever dries out during the dry season. The ashes from the fires are a good corrective for the acid soil. Then they plant such crops as abaca, bananas, papayas, corn, and coffee, which can be cultivated between the logs and around the stumps. This is the kind of farming which the administration has urged, but it has been difficult to get men steeped in the traditions of lowland rice culture to follow a radically different type of agriculture.

The farmers from Leyte and Samar and to some extent those from Luzon had been accustomed to the destruction of ty-phoons, to the inroads of locusts and of various plant pests. These old enemies gave no trouble in Mindanao, but the settlers found themselves pitted against new enemies: the wild pigs, rats, and monkeys that lived in the jungle. The rats gnawed through the stalk of the rice plant near the base, then ate the fallen grain.[1] Monkeys came in chattering parties and feasted royally on the tender part of the immature rice whenever a crop was left unguarded. The worst enemies of all were the wild pigs. In one night they would riddle a field of *camotes* (sweet potatoes). They easily knocked down corn and rice and even destroyed young coconut trees. Possessed of a keen sense of smell, they were difficult to stalk; they were also daring in their attack. The rattle of tin cans or the clacking of a bamboo noise-maker would drive off monkeys on a moonlight night, but the wild pigs required more strenuous measures. They were diffi-cult to trap; they could be cornered by dogs and killed with spears if one had both skill and courage. The best way to get rid of them was by hunting with shotguns, but the ex-Huks first must convince the army that they would use the ammunition only on the wild animals of the jungle. In the meantime, hunt-ing with firearms is limited to the soldiers. Fencing is possible, but too expensive. The settlers hoped that they could save most of their crops through constant vigilance and that ultimately the clearing of the jungle would drive the wild pigs from the area.

Many of the settlers faced a problem of difficult terrain. Much of the level land at Kapatagan, which looked ideal dur-ing the dry season, stood in water six inches to a foot deep when the rains came, and the farm roads were quagmires. The farm administration has put several hundred pesos into drainage ditches to make the road passable. Ultimately, lateral ditches will lower the water level on the farmland to the desired point. The problem is not insoluble, but it still needs attention.

At Buldon some of the farm lots are cluttered with large rocks, and the settlers have rolling land and steep hillsides. One settler complained that he had "fallen out of his farm five times," but not all the farms are this steep. Some of the worst lots in the original draw were rejected, and there have been some reassignments to land with more favorable terrain. Coffee is recommended at Buldon as the basic permanent crop. The sloping hillsides are ideal for its culture, but it will take time for the flatlanders to realize that hillside farming has its own virtues.

The distance between townsite and farm lots and the difficulty of river crossings cause the settlers much trouble. Especially is this true at Buldon, where the Simuay River cuts a
deep gash between the town and the farms, and then swings
eastward and cuts off the more distant farm lots a second time.
One of the settlers from that area had a narrow escape from
drowning after the last harvest. A heavy wooden bridge has
been built at the crossing near the town, but the river near his
farm is still unspanned. After a rain the water rose and rushed
through its channel with a noisy roar. Against the advice of
neighbors he tried to cross on foot with a sack of grain on his
head. The grain was swept downstream, and the settler barely
saved his own life.

Even the bridge at Buldon offers a problem. The life ex-
pectancy of a wooden bridge across these mountain streams in
Mindanao is two to three years. The one at Buldon EDCOR
Farm is already leaning; the top rail on the side against the current was lost in the last high water. During floods the river rolls
huge boulders down its bed. These crash against the pilings.
Then logs and brush catch on the bridge and build up tremendous water pressure. As soon as the timbers of the bridge have
begun to rot and weaken, its days are limited. The only permanent solution is a steel span, and this is quite expensive.

A farm without access to the surrounding areas is practically
worthless. Buldon Farm needs a permanent bridge near the
townsite capable of carrying heavy loads; it needs a smaller
one to the outlying farms capable of supporting a carabao and
sled or cart. These are basic to the economic security of the
farm and to the permanency of the community. Settlers said,
"We shall make this our permanent home; but if the government withdraws, we cannot remain." What could the settlers
do by themselves in the face of a washed-out bridge? A ferry by
raft is out of the question because of the huge boulders which
rise above the surface of the water.

At both Kapatagan and Buldon the farms lie to one side of
the town. This means a long, arduous trip from residence to
work for those with outlying lots. One settler complained, "It
takes me half a day to reach my lot. When I arrive I am hot and
tired. After resting, it is time to return home. How can I ever
work?" Many have built shelters on their farm lots so that they

can stay overnight. This reduces the travel back and forth. But if the family has children in school, the wife has to remain in town. Family life is interrupted, the help of the family in the farming is diminished, and the value of sociability in the town is reduced.

When the farms were opened there was a problem of insufficient tools. For example, two months after the first settlers arrived in Buldon there still were not even enough bolos to go around. This hurdle has long since been passed, and there are now plenty of small tools. Today one of the foremost needs of the settlers is for carabaos and plows. Some 33 per cent of them state this as a need, in addition to the 35 per cent who believe that the primary need is heavy machinery to help in land clearing. At the close of 1953 many of the settlers at Kapatagan still had no carabao. One of them said, "We understood when we came that we would be given a carabao. This was not done. All the work is done by hand. I don't know whether they will fulfill this promise."[2] The good name of the administration became linked with the availability of carabaos and plows. At Buldon the farm administrator had only thirty-nine carabaos to assign among two hundred settlers. Those with some areas of cogon grass on their land had first choice, since a plow is of maximum usefulness in cultivating the grassy turf. Of the thirty-nine settlers with carabaos, only twenty-two had plows. The EDCOR administration is fully aware of this problem. For months a sum had been appropriated for the purchase of carabaos and plows, but the funds had not been released. At year's end there still was no money to meet this need.

Early in 1954 when President Magsaysay banned the butchering of carabaos in order to increase the nation's supply of work animals the government found itself with some one hundred animals on its hands. The order came to ship them to EDCOR. When the coming of the carabaos was announced, the settlers gathered and waited until they arrived long after dark. Finally they came, weak and half starved from the long journey. Some of the animals were too small for heavy plowing. Next day a discouraged settler brought his carabao back to the farm administrator, explaining, "Sir, I put my hand on his back, and he fell over." EDCOR still has a problem of securing work animals. The ex-Huks are trying to carve farms out of the jungle without private capital for support, and with the aid of a government which is doing its best but which has very limited funds.

In addition to the economic problems, the settlers face other questions of a social nature that are equally serious to them. Young families, where the wife is closely confined to the care of infants and small children, have only the husband available for farm work unless there are other relatives in the household. Single men are also handicapped on the farm by lack of the available labor supply of a family. This problem has been met partly through co-operative exchange of labor. Where group labor is essential in clearing and harvesting, friends and neighbors join forces and help each other.

Widow Romano has a particularly difficult family problem. She has seven children; the eldest, sixteen, is the only one out of school and able to work on the farm; the youngest is under two. She and her husband had been farmers in Iloilo when he joined the Huks after the war. A year later in 1949 she also joined the dissidents. Capadocia, the top commander, had sent word that he needed her. Partly out of fear and partly out of the sense of adventure she went.

It was three months before she managed to see her husband. In the meantime she had completed a course of indoctrination at a Huk training center and had been placed in charge of an organizing committee. She traveled from barrio to barrio with her committee, enlisting new recruits and collecting supplies. Later she worked at one of the production bases in the mountains.

Early one morning in May 1951 an outpost guard rushed through the camp shouting that the government troops were all around the place. Before the Huks could escape, firing broke out. A young girl lying near Romano was killed. When the firing stopped, those left ran into a near-by thicket. Romano lay bleeding and wounded from a shot through the pelvis. Shortly afterward the soldiers found her and captured her. Her husband, who was absent at the time of this raid, was killed several months later in a similar skirmish across the mountains.

After her recovery from the wound, Romano volunteered to go to EDCOR in Mindanao. The Buldon EDCOR community has been a good place to rear her children, but the family is still far from self-supporting. This season their rice crop was destroyed by the wild pigs because there was no one to guard it at night. What chance of success has a penniless widow with seven children in a pioneer settlement in Mindanao? How many years will it be before her children are old enough to develop a self-supporting farm? And how many more years will it take the family to repay its debt to the government? Should EDCOR refuse to take such families? Or does the rehabilitation of the family of an ex-Huk and the education of the children justify the government's investment?

Paulino Delfin at fifty-five years of age is one of the oldest men at Buldon. He has no wife and no children, but he lived with a nephew who helped him on the farm until the boy was ambushed and killed by a Moro neighbor. Tension ran high. The government's experiment in land settlement for ex-Huks might have been wrecked in a Moro-Christian war.

When the farm lots were surveyed at Buldon, some were claimed by Moros on the basis of traditional family holdings. These claims were recognized, and the EDCOR administration even helped the Moros to secure land titles. Relations between the Christians and Mohammedans, which are always volatile, seemed to be peaceful. In one case, however, a mistake was made and an EDCOR settler was assigned to a piece of land claimed by a Moro. This was the lot adjacent to that of Delfin. The farm administrator decided that the claim was valid, and the settler was given another assignment. Furthermore, the Moro was promised a title to his land. Weeks passed and the title still did not arrive. The explanation that these matters take time, sometimes a year or more, made little impression on the Moro, who had no knowledge of legal processes. All he knew was that his land holding had been threatened and that hated Christians were moving in on all sides.

In April 1953 the Moro took his gun and stalked a settler work party in a near-by field. Firing at random, he missed everyone except the mother-in-law of one of the settlers. She was wounded. The Moro dropped out of sight for a couple of weeks. Then on May 2 he sneaked into the Delfin farm lot and shot and killed Paulino's nephew.

This incident nearly precipitated civil war between the settlers and their Moro neighbors. Only the firm control of Major Valenova, experienced in handling Moro problems, prevented a disastrous outbreak of violence. As months passed the atmosphere quieted, but the Moro outlaw is still at large. The settlers, especially those living near Moro farms, are fearful of an ambush. Some still refuse to go to their lots without an armed guard. The presence of an army unit will probably be needed in this area for several years to come in order that the necessary security may be provided for peaceful development of the land.

Trying to clear the jungle largely with hand tools, farming in many instances without benefit of carabao or plow, lacking needed capital, facing difficult family situations, and worrying over the prospect of a Moro outbreak, especially if the army should withdraw—these were the problems that concerned the settlers as they began the year 1954.

CHAPTER SIX

ADMINISTRATIVE PROBLEMS

Desirable and unclaimed land in the Philippines is practically impossible to find, even in areas supposedly reserved by the government. This situation was the root cause of many of the problems of the farm administration. No sooner had the EDCOR surveying and construction teams begun work than they ran afoul of the ancestral claims of Moros and the squatter claims of other Filipinos. In the years before the war settlers had begun to push into the Kapatagan plain and established small farms. None secured a land title. During the lawless years of the war they had been driven out and were afraid to return. But when the army moved in, laid out a townsite, and established a permanent garrison, the squatters returned and took up their claims. Slim though the evidence was, most of the claims were granted both to squatters and to Moros. Out of the 205 lots surveyed for the Kapatagan project, 11 went to Moros and 68 of the choicest ones near the townsite went to squatters. This meant that the EDCOR settlers had to take the more distant farms.

The same story was repeated at Buldon except that the civilian claims were scattered and not bunched near the town. Months after the community had been founded the farm administration was still having to defend itself against the action of squatters who, often with the connivance of shyster lawyers, were filing suits in the courts of Cotabato Province.[1]

The loss of lots to prior claimants had two important negative results. First, it meant a sizable reduction in the number of farms available to ex-Huks. Second, administrative costs per settler were increased, since the same personnel and functions had to be maintained for the smaller group as would have been required for a larger one. However, on the positive side, the recognition of squatter claims created good will for EDCOR in the surrounding country and materially hastened the acceptance of the newcomers by the neighboring inhabitants.

One squatter at Kapatagan has been especially annoying and difficult. He appeared on the farm lot of settler Florencio

72

Ramirez in June 1952 and proceeded to build a hut and start clearing the land. Ramirez, who had fought with the Huks in Central Luzon, protested to the squatter and to the farm administration. Captain Jongko offered the man another lot in an attempt to solve the problem peacefully, but he declined and filed a claim in court. Summoned by the farm administration to a conference, he refused to appear. Soldiers had to be sent to bring him for consultation. All attempts to appeal to reason and common sense failed. Ramirez continued to clear one side of the farm while the squatter cleared the other. When the case finally reached the Bureau of Lands, the decision was in favor of Ramirez. The director wrote the squatter to vacate. The farm administration thought this was the end of the matter, but weeks passed and the squatter did not budge. He was still there in October 1953, sixteen months after he first settled himself. How patient should an administration be?

To keep the relations between the settlers and the Moros in good order has required constant attention. The Moros, especially those in the area of Buldon, were apprehensive about their land. They felt that they were being crowded out. Although they may have cultivated only a hectare or two in a wide forest, they thought of the whole jungle as theirs. In an effort to prevent misunderstanding, the governor of Cotabato and the mayor of Parang, themselves educated Moros, came to Buldon to explain the EDCOR program and allay fears. This was generally successful. Even so, there was one instance at Buldon when a Moro attacked several work parties and killed one of the settlers.

The only bloodshed at Kapatagan occurred when a band of thirty Moro outlaws ambushed and killed a soldier on the road three kilometers from the farm. But in this case the offenders were outsiders and as much feared and disliked by the Kapatagan Moros as by the settlers.

The farm administrator's efforts to help the Moros have not always been accepted. At Buldon, Major Valenova sent notices to all the Moro farmers within the project boundaries that the EDCOR office would be happy to help them fill out application papers for land titles. Some took advantage of this service, but one decided that he would circumvent all the red tape. He hired a lawyer at the considerable expense of ₱100 for the purpose of securing a paper that would show that he owned the land. A few weeks later the Moro had his paper and brought it around to show the major. It was a tax declaration! The Moro became very angry when he was told this, and threatened to kill the lawyer who had tricked him. But Major Valenova said, "Don't do that. You have what you asked for. The paper states that this is your land and is subject to the following taxes. But it is not a land title. Why didn't you come to the office and fill out application forms for a land title? The service is free." The Moro, humbled by so many complications, replied, "But, Sir, I am only an ignorant Moro." The major would have readily assented, though he wisely refrained from putting the thought into words. Much of the problem was born of the utter ignorance of a simple people when confronted with the complicated legal processes of civilized society.

One morning the brother of the Moro Datu* who donated the townsite at Buldon came to the farm administrator and asked for an army truck to haul some lumber. The major explained that the army equipment could not be used for special private hauling. The Moro was insistent. He felt that he should receive special consideration and favors. Furthermore, he said that the army truck had hauled rice to Cotabato for the Datu. "Yes," answered the major, "but that was part of our regular trip to the city and therefore cost the army nothing extra. We are very short on gasoline and cannot make a special trip for non-army purposes." Seeing that the Moro was becoming very angry, Valenova sent for an army captain who was a Moro and asked him to explain the situation in the man's own dialect. Finally they reached an agreement whereby the Moro paid for the gasoline, and the truck hauled his lumber. Such are the delicate human problems which constantly beset the administration.

East of the EDCOR farm at Kapatagan is an area large enough to double that held at present by the settlers. It is owned by a Moro and occupied by him and his five brothers. They cultivate only a fraction of the land.[2] The farm administrator has tried to persuade the Moro to give the land to the government for the expansion of the EDCOR project, keeping of course a

* A Moro Datu is a chieftain who is looked upon as the head of his clan or village.

surveyed farm for himself and one for each of the five brothers. The Moros would receive the advantages of living in a well-developed community with roads, schools, medical care, and a market for their farm products. Negotiations dragged along. Captain Jongko invited the Moros to come look at a map of the proposed development, and they could select the areas they wished to keep for themselves. When the day arrived the five brothers were present, but the one who owned the land failed to appear. Each of the brothers indicated on the map the part he wished for himself. When they were through, there was nothing left for EDCOR. The conversations were dropped.

The EDCOR administration has always had to scrounge for adequate financial support for its projects, which were started with no appropriations and with volunteer labor. The Kapatagan farm was opened and carried through the first six months of its development on ₱320,000; the newly opened project in Isabela Province has cost even less. A much larger EDCOR farm has been planned for a new site in Cotabato Province. An appropriation to construct a road to the area, streets, and farm roads, cottages, and central buildings, though more adequate than previous ones, still totals only ₱1,200,000.[3] This is about the sum of the gate receipts for one of the World Series baseball games in New York City. Half that amount would provide adequately for all the costs of operating one of the EDCOR farms for an entire year. They have been getting along on much less.

In the last quarter of 1953 the lack of adequate financial support required that the work on certain projects be curtailed. The drainage program at Kapatagan was limited to the main road; lateral roads were still impassable by truck. Carabaos and plows needed by the settlers could not be purchased, though an order for them had long been on the books. There was no supply of diesel fuel at Buldon to operate the two bulldozers and a road grader. While farm roads were badly needed, equipment stood idle. Gasoline to operate the supply trucks was short. The farm administrator hoped the gasoline would last long enough to bring in the planting materials needed by the settlers. The motor pool in charge of the maintenance of vehicles was constantly short of spare parts.

Finally, the administration had to cut the ration allowance to the settlers. This worked no universal hardship, since some of the settlers were already self-supporting and others were partially so. In some instances the cut in rations would serve as a goad to increased efforts to make the farms produce. But there were a few cases where illness, or loss of a crop, had left the family with few resources. The farm administrator needed more funds to help in these emergencies.

The work of the farm administrator has been greatly complicated by the promises, often exaggerated, which were made to prospective settlers before they came to the farm. Civil Affairs officers, area commanders, congressmen, the Social Welfare Department, and the Department of National Defense were all recruiting settlers and sending in applications. In their enthusiasm for the new program they sometimes promised more than could be delivered. The EDCOR administration was supposed to interview all applicants and approve them. But during the early months of getting organized, the interviews at EDCOR headquarters did not correct the glowing promises which had been made to the settlers. As a matter of fact, a mimeographed circular entitled "The EDCOR Project," which was sent to all army units for purposes of publicity and recruiting, was responsible for the idea that the farming would be done with mechanized equipment. The pamphlet read, "With the aid of EDCOR farm machinery and technical assistance from its personnel, an initial one to three hectares of each settler's farm will be cleared and cultivated depending upon each settler's capabilities for work. . . . The settler may continue receiving services from the agricultural machinery pool after he has acquired his farm lot for a nominal charge." This type of mechanized assistance EDCOR has never been able to offer, but many of the settlers still strongly believe that the administration should help them clear the land.

In the name of EDCOR one politician made promises of free rations, free houses, cleared land, and tractor farming. On this basis he gathered a motley collection of older adolescents, the problem boys of the province, and sent them to Buldon. Such an orientation to the realities of jungle farming could lead only to the failure of this group.

One of the most troublesome problems of the administration grew out of the fact that it did not have complete control over the selection of settlers: it could not entirely weed out the unfit prior to their arrival and it could not control their unrealistic anticipations about life at the farm. Keenly aware of these difficulties, Colonel Mirasol has insisted on a much more careful recruiting and sifting of applicants for the newer projects. He said, "The psychological propaganda of offering the settlers everything was unwise. It was too easily misunderstood and it gave the settlers an insufficient challenge. Now we take every applicant separately. We find out what tools he has, whether he has a carabao, and what other resources. Then we promise only to meet the needs he himself cannot fill. The settler then knows he must work hard because he has put his own resources into the project."

Another problem concerns the authority of the local farm administrator. According to army orders, the complaints of the settlers were to be handled at the local level. Colonel Mirasol has made every effort to strengthen the authority of the officers on the farms, but in actual practice the settlers have gone over the heads of the farm administrator to the central headquarters at Camp Murphy or to higher government authorities. Certain incidents at the farms encouraged the settlers to think they could get special privileges by appealing to "the higher-ups." For example, a high government official visiting the farm was warmly greeted by one of the settlers. They had formerly been acquaintances. After the handshaking and pleasantries, the settler asked the official for chicken wire and an incubator so that he could go into the poultry business. Turning to the farm administrator, the official said, in effect, "Give him anything he wants. See that he gets it, for I shall be back in a month to check up." This conversation took place in the presence of a large gathering of settlers and put the farm administrator in a most embarrassing position. He had no money for such special projects, and could not in any case afford to play favorites among the settlers. Such incidents seriously undermined his authority.

EDCOR has been remarkably successful with its settlers. Failures have been few. Only nineteen cases, or 6 per cent of the total number of settlers at the end of 1953, had left the projects or been dismissed. Six of these were convicted of theft; five refused to work and develop their farms; three deserted; two were found in illegal possession of firearms; two resigned because of poor health; one tried to incite trouble against the government. For these various reasons they were dropped.

The farm administrators are reluctant to dismiss a settler. They give him every opportunity and encouragement, because they wish to succeed in the basic purpose of reforming ex-Huks. Colonel Mirasol, in a letter to the farm administrators, stated:

"It has been observed that there is a growing number of settlers who are being recommended for dropping as a result of misbehavior or laziness. Although such action is fully justified in accordance with existing policy, this administrative action should be regarded only as a last resort purely for the protection of the interest of the government and the well-being of the EDCOR project.

"Actually the rehabilitation of the expelled settler under EDCOR has failed every time such a discharge occurs.

"It is, therefore, necessary to make a study of these sociological problems in order to arrive at a realistic solution, if such a solution is still possible, so that the rehabilitation of the settler, particularly ex-Huks, may be carried out to a successful conclusion."

However, if a settler has violated his contract, as in the few cases cited above, he is dismissed. In instances where the settler does not take an interest in his work, the administrator may first send him a warning letter. In half of the fourteen cases who have received such letters, this first warning has been sufficient. The others received a second warning, which in effect put them on probation and gave them three months to show positive improvement. At the end of that period, those showing no progress are subject to an investigation. Only two settlers were in this stage of ejection in November of 1953. A verdict of unworthiness by the investigating board leads to dismissal.

A few individuals who found themselves grossly unsuited for farm work signed requests to be returned to their provinces before their cases came up for investigation. This was true of a young man, eighteen years of age, from Leyte. He arrived with the last of the settlers to come to Buldon, in January 1953. He was assigned a house, a home lot, a farm about five kilometers from the town, and was given a ration amounting to ₱1.20 a day. In addition, the project supervisor gave him instruction and encouragement, but he did not work. He complained that his farm was too far away and too rugged, but others were doing well on land even farther away and more mountainous. He appeared to be immature and uninterested. After six months he asked to be returned to Leyte, where he promised to work and pay back the ₱320 debt he had incurred with EDCOR.

The failures on the EDCOR farms were young men, averaging twenty-five years of age. Fewer than half of them (42 per cent) were married, and the average number of dependents was two. They came from many provinces and from various regions in the Philippines. Those who had held jobs previously had worked as farmers, fishermen, sawyers, stevedores, policemen, and drivers. Their average school attainment was the third grade. Among all these characteristics, youth and immaturity, lack of family responsibilities, poor education, and a record of waywardness before coming to EDCOR accounted for most of the failures.

Every month each settler is given a rating with respect to co-operation, efficiency and industry, and character and conduct. For example, concerning co-operation, a rating of one means "exceptionally successful in working with others"; two, "works in harmony with others"; three, "co-operates fairly well"; four, "difficult to adjust, unco-operative." In similar fashion the settlers are rated from one to four on efficiency and industry, and on character and conduct. Using the combined scores for each individual, the author divided the settlers into three groups: superior, average, and problem settlers. The superior group made up 16 per cent of the total; the average group, 73 per cent; and the problem cases, 11 per cent. The characteristics of each of these groups were then examined in order to discover what makes a successful settler and what leads to problem behavior.

The most successful adjustments were made by the older and more mature men. The average age for the superior group was thirty-seven years; for the average group, thirty-one years; and for the problem settlers, twenty-five years. Apparently, the best age for pioneering is during a man's thirties.

The findings concerning superior adjustment and age were reinforced by the figures on marriage. Some 81 per cent of those with a superior rating were married and 62 per cent of the average settlers were, but only 25 per cent of the problem group were married. Clearly, a man heading out to clear the jungle needs a wife.

Furthermore, his chances of success are greater if he has a large number of dependents, preferably old enough to work. Disregarding the age of dependents and including in-laws as well as children, the superior settlers had an average of five dependents; the average group, three; and the problem cases, two. A family generates a sense of responsibility, and the larger the household the greater the sense of security and family morale. At least this is true on the frontier in Mindanao.

The commonly held opinion that settlers should be chosen from among those with a farm background was not borne out by the facts. Among the superior group 38 per cent had no previous farm experience, while 22 per cent among the average group and only 19 per cent of the problem cases lacked farm background. Although there are individual exceptions, previous farm experience was not essential to success at EDCOR. The rigid folkways of the old agricultural areas tend to prevent a man from ready acceptance of the different methods required to farm on the frontier.

In the main, the better educated men have made the better record at EDCOR. The average school attainment of the superior group was the fifth grade; the settlers making an average adjustment were third-grade level; while the problem group had on an average only second-grade education. However, in every group—superior, average, and problem—there were illiterates with no schooling. College graduates were found with both superior and average ratings. Within the problem group were a few cases of high-school graduates. But in spite of these occasional exceptions, the more educated man has a greater chance of becoming a successful settler.

In terms of their relation to the Huk movement, who make the best settlers? Those who were deeply involved in the Huk movement, the stabilizers, or those on the fringe of the revolution? It was a common impression among the EDCOR officials that the "real ex-Huks" make the best settlers. However, an analysis of the settlers according to their adjustment at the farm does not bear this out. All the settlers were divided into four groups: the stabilizers, the captured Huks, the surrendered Huks, and the suspects. Using the official ratings of the farm administration, an average for each of the groups was figured on a scale varying from 3 to 12, the lower score indicating the superior rating. If the real ex-Huks made better settlers, their score should be lower than the others. Here are the results:

Stabilizer group . . .	6.1
Captured Huks . . .	7.0
Surrendered Huks . .	7.3
Suspects	7.3

The stabilizer group showed up better than the others. This was to be expected, for they were more carefully selected. Statistically, the difference between the 7.0 and the 7.3 is insignificant. The only conclusion justified is that being a captured, or surrendered, or suspected Huk in itself made no difference in successful adjustment at the EDCOR farms.

The EDCOR administration makes no sweeping claims of success. Colonel Mirasol said, "We don't take for granted that the job is done when the settler is happy, or when he is prosperous. The real task is to see that he is weaned away from communist ideas. We cannot always judge a settler by what he says and does. The best spies make the best collaborators." Through an intelligence system the settlers are classified as red, white, or blue. The reds are those who must be watched; the whites are safe and harmless; the blues could be trusted with firearms in an emergency. The EDCOR bends its efforts to moving individuals along the course from red to blue.

The danger of Huk agents in the surrounding area, fomenting trouble and sabotaging the project, is always real. Plots by Communist cell groups against the Kapatagan farm have been discovered and thwarted. One EDCOR settler was dismissed for fomenting antigovernment activity. These plots have been few and not extensive; in fact, EDCOR has suffered less disturbance on the score of disloyalty than was expected.

The EDCOR has accumulated a wealth of experience concerning land settlement with ex-revolutionaries. When Captain Jongko, who has guided the Kapatagan farm from its inception, was asked to state the principles he would employ if he were beginning again, he listed the following:

1. The land should be thoroughly and carefully inspected and all squatters removed or their claims adjusted before the settlement begins.

2. The townsite should cover about eighty hectares and be located centrally where all farm roads converge.

3. There should be an L-5 landing strip within the project in order to provide contact with the nearest military establishment.

4. The survey of farm lots in six-hectare plots should be completed before the settlers arrive.

5. Settlers should be carefully screened to find those suited for farm life. They should be told that they will have to clear land covered by forests. All arrangements should be understood correctly from the beginning.

6. The engineers should first ensure a safe water supply and construct a power plant for electric lights.

7. A dispensary and medical service should be established immediately.

8. Settlers should be granted a ration but on the clear understanding that it must be paid back.

9. Money crops, such as abaca and coffee, should be planted in addition to rice and corn.

10. When all the settlers have acquired land titles, any indebtedness should be turned over to the Philippine National Bank for collection.

11. Army personnel should be used in opening settlements for several reasons: one, the problem of security on the frontier is a military policing job; two, a working army is less expensive in the long run than a "standing" army; and three, the army's system of accounting and discipline leads to rapid and efficient progress.

12. Personnel assigned to EDCOR should be officers and men who have volunteered and who are inspired by missionary zeal for the job.

The experience of EDCOR has underscored the importance of roads which give the settlers ready access to the outside communities. Other essentials to successful pioneering proved to be security of life through adequate police protection; an orderly, reliable process of granting land titles; provision for health, education, and religion; and just enough assistance to help a settler become self-supporting but not so much that his will to work is destroyed.

At EDCOR the Filipino genius for administration is amply demonstrated. Perhaps by the more rigid and impersonal standards of American efficiency the settlements would be criticized as loose-jointed operations. Perhaps in the same length of time an American efficiency expert would have moved more dirt, dug more ditches, constructed more farm roads, and cleared more jungle. But he would also have spent much more money. Within the means at their disposal the farm administrators have kept the projects in sound economic condition and have clung doggedly to the basic purpose of creating healthy democratic communities. Considering their human material, the diversity of backgrounds, the high illiteracy, and the Huk orientation, the achievement is remarkable. The administrators have shown understanding, sympathy, and above all patience. In these essentially oriental qualities they have excelled.

These administrative qualities and principles have been developed through experience by a responsible government. They may sound unexciting and prosaic in comparison with the high-sounding claims and promises of Communist revolutionaries, but they represent real achievement. A revolutionary group, such as the Huks, who are unburdened with the machinery of government, possesses an unavoidable propaganda advantage. While the government in power must wrestle with all the problems involved in making a social system work, its opponents are free to criticize mistakes, concentrate on weak spots, and paint extravagant pictures of what they would do if they were in control. The thoughtless citizen may sometimes turn his back on the solid, if at times halting, progress of his government to grasp at the elusive promises of an agitator. In the war against communism the democracies must always make a case for the substance of administrative effort against the shadow of the revolutionist's dream. Here lay the strategic value of EDCOR.

CHAPTER SEVEN

HURDLING CLASS LINES

Pedro Mariano had always lived on a farm. His earliest memories were of games played along the narrow dikes which divided the rice paddies and of trips to the water hole to bring the carabao. How he loved this big gentle companion! By holding her tail he could climb up behind and take a ride on her broad friendly back. The carabao would flap her ears and plod along as if she had complete understanding of the needs of small boys.

When Pedro grew up he helped with the rice planting. As a child he had carried the young shoots from the seed bed to the field. Now he did a man's work: plowing through the soft deep mud before the planting, setting out the young seedlings, taking a turn at guard while the grain ripened, and working through the long days of harvest. He labored beside his four brothers and two sisters and his parents. His father was a tenant farmer working on the customary fifty-fifty crop-sharing arrangement. He had four hectares of land, which exceeded the average two to three hectares per tenant in his province. And yet this was not enough—not enough to keep the boys, now men, employed; and not enough to support the family.

At the beginning of each planting season the landlord furnished the tenant with two sacks of palay (unhusked rice) for seed. Any grain which the tenant received in excess of this was a loan to be repaid at the end of the harvest. The family always had to borrow to piece out a meager existence. For every sack of palay loaned, the landlord collected double at harvest time. But in addition he figured in the change of price of palay during this interim. Invariably the price was twice as high when the tenant borrowed during the time of scarcity as when he paid it back at harvest. Thus, instead of collecting double, the landlord collected quadruple interest for the six-months period. In terms of a year this meant an interest rate of 800 per cent. This is the problem of usury, the most pernicious and vexatious aspect of the agrarian trouble in Central Luzon.

As Pedro grew to maturity and the family went deeper and

84

deeper into debt, he determined to leave home and find a job. First he tried the naval base at Olongapo, then he made the rounds in Manila. Discouraged, he returned home to the farm. Then he heard about a job in Iloilo and made the long and expensive boat trip there, only to meet further disappointment. Back in Manila, he met a friend who invited him to lunch at a bar in Tondo, a slum area. As Pedro related his story of failures, the friend said, "You have no work; there is no sense in slaving as a tenant farmer for a starvation share; why not join the Huks?" Thus Pedro, like many others from the rice lands of Central Luzon, became a revolutionary. He determined to fight against a system that did not reward hard work and which provided no opportunities for youth.

Such agrarian unrest constitutes the background and motivation of 32 per cent of the ex-Huks at the EDCOR farms. Yet the simple fact of economic exploitation is only the most obvious and dramatic expression of the system of social classes that has long characterized Philippine society. As the statistic of 32 per cent indicates, the source of unrest which feeds the Huk revolt is far more varied and complex than economic exploitation of the poor peasant. The fundamental problem is a stratified society where people are divided into classes with privileges and rewards unequally distributed among them. Not only economic goods, but recognition, prestige, educational opportunities, voting power, and equality before the law are at stake. Interviews with ex-Huks at EDCOR made abundantly clear that they resented bitterly being low man on the social totem pole.

The social system in the rural Philippines, which comprises some 76 per cent of the total population of the nation,[1] includes two main classes, the landlords and the tenants. The money-lenders and the overseers are a part of the landowning class. The Philippine Army and the Constabulary form a third group, theoretically a neutral force to protect the equal rights of citizens under the law; but in actual practice their power has been used largely to support the interests of the landlords. Whether justifiably or not, tenants from Central Luzon have a deep fear and distrust of the Constabulary which is passed along from parents to children. Confronted with a choice of "protection" by the Constabulary or life under the Huks, many chose the latter.

The landlords are a wealthy leisure class; they live in large, beautiful houses and drive big automobiles. Much of their time is spent in Manila or on vacations abroad. They can afford many servants and expensive educations for their children. The tenants, on the other hand, never travel far from their homes. They possess little or no formal education, for even the minimum fees charged in Philippine public schools place a strain on their resources. They work hard and grow old at an early age. Malaria and dysentery and a poor diet take a heavy toll. The difference between the classes is sharp; the social distance is like a wide abyss.

The present social system has a long history of development. The landlords of today are descendants of the *caciques,* the wealthy aristocrats of the Spanish period; while the tenant farmers occupy the same position as the *aparceros,* or peasants, of former times. Under Spanish rule the Civil Guard was the terror of the countryside and the barrios.[2] The Constabulary seems to have inherited some of the bitterness which had developed toward that former police force.

The class structure of the Spanish regime has some similarities to that of the pre-Spanish period and did in fact assimilate some of the elements of the earlier social organization. At the time the Spaniards established themselves in the Philippines, there was already a well-developed social system among the inhabitants of the islands. The governing head of each village was a Datu, or chief, who, together with his family, occupied the top social position in the community. Beneath the Datu and his family were three classes: free men, share tenants, and slaves. The free-born men in the village were not required to pay taxes or share their produce with the chief, but they were obligated to support him in war and to assist in the cultivation of his fields and in the building and repair of his house. The next class owned their own dwellings but had to share half their produce with their master. Those in the lowest class lived in their owner's house or in a dwelling provided by him. They could not marry without permission and could be sold at any time.[3] Persons were enslaved in several ways: some were captives from intertribal wars; some were children of slaves and considered as wards of their masters; others were servants in perpetuity as a result of debts for which their labor was never considered sufficient and complete payment.[4]

During the Spanish period and afterward, slavery diminished until it all but disappeared. However, there has been some persistence in modern times of the practice of keeping individuals in a condition of semipermanent servitude on the basis of unpaid family debts.[5] The customary fifty-fifty crop division is still the basic arrangement between landlord and tenant, although recent legislative efforts to revise and improve the position of the tenant date from the prewar "social justice" program of the Commonwealth Government.[6] During the long years of the Spanish rule most of the free born villagers in Central Luzon lost their independent-farmer status and became tenants first on the *encomiendas* (land-grant estates) and then, after their abolition at the beginning of the seventeenth century, on the Church estates or on the increasing land holdings of the *caciques.* Thus, in the course of a social process which spread over several generations, the freemen as a group largely disappeared into the ranks of the share tenants. Meanwhile, the Spaniards had recognized the native village leadership and made use of these leading families as a means of governing and maintaining control. The ruling families among the Filipinos intermarried with the Spaniards and ultimately became the *caciques,* or landed aristocracy.[7] By the time of the arrival of the Americans in 1900 the rural Philippines had developed a two-class system composed of the landed aristocracy at the top and the share tenant at the bottom. This division with its attendant injustices and agrarian unrest persisted during the American period in spite of plans and occasional attempts at land reform.[8]

The EDCOR farms have not been immune to the influence of this social system in Philippine rural society. Thus, in the EDCOR communities are found three distinct classes: the officers, whose status approximates that of the landlord; the settlers, whose status is similar to that of the tenant; and the enlisted men, who occupy the traditional position of the policemen. The class system at EDCOR is similar to and yet it is not identical with that on the outside. The farm administrator is not in truth a landlord; the settlers are not tenants; the enlisted men are more than mere policemen. But the social conditioning in the former society had developed attitudes in regard to each of the classes which have been carried over into the EDCOR experiment and have hampered the growth of a democratic community. The settlers often feel that they are being treated like tenants, and the administration is set apart as if it were an elite class.

No evidence of class distinction is possible at EDCOR on the basis of type of housing, since all the dwellings are about alike. Each of the three groupings, however, lives in a separate area. For example, at Buldon the enlisted men occupy houses near the road at the entrance of the townsite. They serve as a buffer between the Christian settlement and the Moros in the adjacent barrio. On the first main street and facing the administration building are the officers' homes. Behind these on other streets are houses of the settlers. Some degree of physical segregation is an inevitable accompaniment of class divisions.

Relationships between the three classes are cordial even while the distinctions between them are being maintained. Some of the settlers' wives send special dishes of food or help to serve the table when the officers are entertaining guests at the farm. On special occasions the settlers elected to the town council are invited to meet visiting guests at the officers' dining hall, but they either decline to eat or else wait until the second table is served.

It is appropriate for the enlisted men to entertain the officers, but not the other way around. An enlisted man's family at Buldon invited the officers to dinner in celebration of the butchering of a cow. At the first serving were the officers of highest rank. Other officers ate at the second sitting; enlisted men, third; and women, last. When officers and guests visit the settlers on their farms, the settlers graciously serve food, such as fruit or boiled eggs. These are pleasant social occasions for all, but there is no similar entertainment of the settlers by the officer class. With the exception of special celebrations of religious holidays, the anniversary of the founding of EDCOR, and the town fiesta, the recreation of the community follows class lines. Only the officers play tennis, on courts that they themselves maintain. Dances are also largely confined to the officer families, although some of the enlisted men play musical instruments on such occasions.

There is, however, much mixing between the settlers and the enlisted men, and there have been some marriages between members of these two groups. Whereas the officers maintain their social distance and their separateness as a class, the settlers and soldiers find much in common, once the fear of the man in uniform has worn off. Many of the settlers have an education equal or superior to that of the enlisted men. As landowners and as possible officeholders in the community the settlers have achieved a status which is the envy even of the officers. The settlers and soldiers are closely enough matched to be competitors. Some of the settlers resent the fact that the soldiers may carry arms, while they are forbidden their use. On the other hand, the soldiers tend to resent work on projects that benefit the ex-Huks, when they who have been loyal have not been given free land. These rivalries may increase as the farms become more productive and the income of the settlers begins to exceed that of the soldiers.

In the Philippines the personal relations between members of the upper and lower classes are often marked by a benevolent paternalism. When a man from the lower class asks a gift from one of the upper class, the individual in the superior class dares not deny the request. To refuse the poor man a gift would be to cast doubt upon one's ability to bestow the favor, and would call the whole status system into question. The poor as well as the rich expect to play the roles that are suitable to their social positions. They expect to be treated as inferior, to do the hard and dirty jobs, and to be cared for and protected. The system is maintained when the benefactor bestows some favor upon the poor, preferably in such a way that the superiority of the one and the inferiority of the other are emphasized.

Many of the settlers at EDCOR were accustomed to the role of inferiority and to treating superiors as benefactors. At the farm they came to the administrator with their problems in the same way they had gone to the landlord back in their barrios. He was expected to act like a good and benevolent representative of the landed aristocracy. When the farm administrator did not fill these expectations, but followed "a policy of self-help," there was considerable confusion. A request for additional rations might be countered with instruction on planting mongo beans as soon as the palay was harvested in order to increase production and keep down the growth of weeds. When settlers begged for help to clear the land, they were given tools and instruction, and were organized into work parties to clear the land for themselves. The lessons were hard ones, for they ran against a current that had flowed through Philippine society for generations.

Misunderstandings arose on both sides. The settlers accused the officers of being cruel and heartless. Protests were sent to the headquarters at Camp Murphy against the inhuman treatment. One officer was charged with driving the settlers to work and depriving them of their freedom. On the other side, the officers thought the settlers were lazy and not trying to carry out their part of the contract. As long as the attitudes that characterized the old social order still prevailed, settlers and officers alike found it difficult to develop a democratic community characterized by a maximum of individual responsibility and self-reliance.

The stratification of society into social classes sets up hurdles in the path of free communication and complete understanding. For example, one of the most trustworthy of the settlers at Buldon came to Major Valenova during the last rice harvest and complained that the wild pigs had destroyed palay that would have yielded forty sacks of grain, about half of his harvest. This destruction had occurred in spite of the fact that the settler had lived on the farm day and night in an effort to protect the crop. The major turned to an officer and gave an order to have soldiers go to the settler's clearing with shotguns that evening and kill the wild pigs. Some days later the settler was asked about the wild pigs.

"They are terrible," he replied. "We can no longer frighten them away. They come right up near the house and trample plants and uproot our garden. If we only had a shotgun, we could kill them easily."

"What about the soldiers?" asked the interviewer. "Did they not come with shotguns to hunt the pigs?"

"Oh, yes, they came one evening about dark and stayed for a couple of hours. Then they left, saying the mosquitoes were too bad," was the disgusted reply. "I don't see why the administration won't let us have shotguns to protect our crops. Don't they trust us? We are still treated like criminals. What is the sense of encouraging people to work hard and plant crops and then not permit them to have a gun to ward off the wild pigs? I'd be willing to buy my own gun, if they would let me."

This is a good illustration of how a program carefully planned by the administration to protect the settlers and extend aid to them had failed in its execution. The settler had an honest and legitimate need which the farm administrator was quick to recognize. His order to hunt and kill the pigs was sincere. But this concern was not communicated to the two enlisted men who were entrusted with the mission. The concern with the success of the project was shared by the officer class, but only to a small degree by the enlisted men to whom the ex-Huks appeared as rivals. To the settler the actions of the administration were ineffective and nonsensical. He was more determined than ever to distrust those outside his class. As long as the attitudes of each group reflected the separateness of its social class, the community progressed with difficulty.

One of the primary aims of EDCOR was to develop prosperous settlements. This meant that every settler not only must work hard but also must follow an intelligent plan for the development of his farm. Agricultural experts planned the best use of the land and the wisest choice of crops. Army officers experienced in modern farming took charge of the training and direction of the settlers. Sometimes these efforts to help met stiff resistance. Especially difficult to communicate was the idea that land once cleared should never be left unplanted, for it would rapidly revert to grass and jungle growth. The fact that this instruction came from an officer and a member of another social class made it sound like foreign and unreliable advice. The project director at Kapatagan reported that after two years of effort he was just beginning to get across a few simple and basic ideas about farming to some of the settlers. When the administrator gave an order backed by force it was, of course, obeyed without question. When he attempted to instruct the settlers, however, they became suspicious and often chose to disregard the advice. The task of imparting information across class lines, in an atmosphere of confidence and understanding, can be surprisingly difficult. The class lines themselves tend to destroy confidence. The problem is not the difficulty of the ideas but the barriers created by social class. Information can be disseminated most easily by the leaders among the settlers themselves, for then no social barriers to acceptance exist.

Social stratification sets one class over against another and breeds distrust. When many of the plans and suggestions of the administration turned out well, the settlers thought nothing of it. When a man's abaca plants rotted in a marshy part of his Kapatagan farm, the administration received the full blame. One bit of poor advice often was enough to precipitate a flight from modern practice back to the customary farming based on superstition.

Class lines breed suspicion. At Buldon one of the settlers received monthly checks from the Department of National Defense. In a small community where the mail was delivered through many hands such unusual letters could never be kept a secret. The rumors began to spread. Perhaps the man was a spy for the department. The settlers rumored that he was spying on them. The officers on their part were suspicious that he had been planted in the settlement to check up on their activities. These rumors subsided only when it was learned that the settler was being paid for past services rendered to the department.

Recognizing these problems, the EDCOR administration has made a valiant effort to transcend class barriers. Colonel Mirasol sent a memorandum to each project requiring that "Officers' visits to individual settler's homes shall be conducted in a friendly atmosphere, preferably after official working hours, and shall not impose any pecuniary or material burden on the part of the settler being visited." Sensitive to the feelings of the settlers, he added that, "The use of mass meetings and gatherings for purposes of indoctrinating settlers' families in the democratic processes is not advisable. . . . Family problems that may be embarrassing in nature are not expected to be aired during public occasions. Announcements affecting settlers shall be relayed through the PA system so as not to create an impression that settlers are made to assemble for purposes of regimentation and mass indoctrination, a reminder of their former lives under communist methods." Every EDCOR officer was charged with the responsibility to attend to problems whenever they arose and not merely to pass them on to the next officer or enlisted man.[9]

The impression should not be created that the EDCOR communities are torn by class strife. Far from it, they are examples of a Filipino effort to replace an ancient and deeply imbedded social system that pitted landlord against tenant and army against the people. The lingering remains of this old society hinder the birth of a new order, but every group at EDCOR was firmly convinced that the new democratic community is in the making. The public schools are enormously influential. The children of all the families attend the same classes and join together in games on the playground. All parents belong to the PTA, and settlers as well as officers and enlisted men hold offices. The town council is a governing body democratically elected. The co-operative store organized at Buldon includes officers, enlisted men, and settlers. The medical service is free to all alike. There is one church for all the community. The farm administrator is not a remote figurehead, but a participating member of the community. Settlers consult him at any hour of the day or night. Fellow officers are impressed by the fact that the major is always available when needed.

Whatever its failures may have been, the administration through hard work has convinced the settlers of its sincerity and good will. Many of the ex-Huks said, "For the first time we have experienced what a true democracy is like."

EDCOR has kindled the ambition of its settlers. They eagerly discuss future plans:

"I want to clear all my land and become prosperous."

"I want to rear my family and educate my children."

"I want to make a comfortable living and get married."

"I want to educate my children so they can defend their own rights."

"I want to clear all my land and plant it in permanent crops so that I may live well."

"I want to make this my permanent home."

"I want to develop my farm so that I will have something to pass on to my children."

"I plan to start a little store as soon as I save enough."

"I want to succeed here and then buy more land."

"I want to improve my livelihood and help the government."

"I would like to educate my two sons to become a doctor and a lawyer."

"I want to work hard and become independent."

"I want to be the richest settler here."

"I want to become a successful farmer."

"I want to live a peaceful and happy life."

These are not the sentiments of exploited peasants; they are the hopes and ambitions of democratic citizens in pursuit of tangible opportunities.

CHAPTER EIGHT

THE EMERGING COMMUNITY

The development of a community where the settlers work together harmoniously has come only with the passage of time. The early days were marred by jealousies, suspicions, and conflict. Later, as the people entered seriously into the task of wresting a livelihood from the jungle, they developed the confidence in one another that replaced separateness with a community of interest.

The first major obstacle to overcome was the clannishness of the different dialect groups. The settlers at Kapatagan came largely from the Tagalog- and Pampangueño-speaking provinces of Luzon, but a few were from other dialect areas. The second project at Buldon contained even more language diversity. Large groups coming from the Visayan provinces spoke Ilongo, Waray-Waray, or Cebuano, while those from Luzon were divided among the Tagalogs, the Pampangueños, and the Ilocanos. The settlers from these six major dialect areas split into six different factions, hostile and suspicious of each other. Open violence broke out between the two most antagonistic groups, the Ilongos and the Tagalogs. The object of this conflict was an attractive Ilongo widow, known as "the Red Flame of Panay."

Her life with the Huks began on the afternoon of January 2, 1951, in a remote barrio in Iloilo Province. "The Red Flame" at that time was teaching in an elementary school and was about to dismiss her children for the day. Without warning some thirty-five armed men surrounded the building, while four of them approached and demanded that she accompany them to a Huk command post in the mountains. When she refused, they grabbed her roughly and carried her away. Hours later they arrived at the headquarters of a local Huk chieftain, who went by the alias of Kulafu, a name taken from a comic strip hero somewhat equivalent to Edgar Rice Burroughs' Tarzan. Though they always kept a close guard to prevent her escape, the Huks never mistreated her. Gradually she was instructed in the Communist aims and was given a safe and harm-

95

less assignment as head of a medical unit. She was the object of Kulafu's personal attentions. In time his kindness won her, and she became his wife.

In September 1951 Kulafu was killed in a raid by members of the Constabulary forces, and "the Red Flame of Panay" surrendered. Several months later, when the opportunity arose to go to EDCOR, she gladly exchanged the dull existence in an army stockade for the prospects of a new life in Mindanao.

When she arrived at the Buldon EDCOR farm, most of the settlers were young men who were unmarried. In no time at all the attractive young widow had dozens of suitors. Serenaders both singly and in groups paraded their charms outside her window at all hours of the night. The competition was so keen that the suitors divided into gangs along the lines of their native dialects. Four brothers and cousins of the Panay "Flame" moved into her house to give protection. The situation became tense, especially between the Ilongos of Panay and the Tagalogs from Luzon, who felt they were being squeezed out of the courting unfairly.

One night an especially determined Tagalog suitor slipped past the guard and entered the quarters of "the Red Flame" from the back door. But in his haste he stumbled over her brothers. There was a scramble and a fight. Bolos flashed in the moonlight, and the widow screamed in fright. The intruder went out a window and down the road, where he was joined by Tagalog cronies. They returned to uphold the honor of their clan only to meet Ilongo reinforcements just as determined to defend "the Red Flame of Panay."

At this point some soldiers on patrol appeared and quietly took a position between the two belligerent groups. After a while the heated emotions cooled and the men returned to quarters, but for days the atmosphere was tense. Such factional strife threatened to destroy the young community. Then Major Valenova conceived a brilliant plan. Equipped with a guitar, he recruited a mixed group of serenaders including soldiers, Visayans, and Tagalogs. Their songs and good-humored petitions to the attractive widow broke the tension. The whole settlement now laughed and enjoyed the show. In the more peaceful atmosphere a real romance developed. Not many moons later the

widow married a soldier, and "the Red Flame of Panay" became "Mrs. Corporal-of-the-Guard."

Factionalism could not survive the demands of life on the
frontier. A man needed neighbors and friends. Co-operation
yielded high returns in companionship and help on the farm.
Taking advantage of these natural forces the leaders among the
settlers as well as in the farm administration encouraged the development of unity and loyalty to the community. The effort
was highly successful. Simeon Gonzales, ex-Huk and formerly
one of the top commanders on Panay, wrote in the settlers' bulletin in celebration of the first anniversary of the founding of
Buldon EDCOR Farm, "As soon as a settler coming from
Luzon and the Visayas gets inside the premises of the EDCOR
townsite, he is no longer a Pampangan, Tagalog, Ilongo, or
Waray-Waray. He is already an EDCOR citizen with obligations to fulfill as a member of the community."

One of the strongest evidences of the developing community
is found in its economic progress. Take the case of Eusebio
Montano, forty-three years of age, who brought his wife and
eight children to EDCOR in February 1951. The Montanos
had been tenant farmers in the rice lands of Central Luzon before they were caught up in the Huk activities. When they arrived at EDCOR their total assets amounted to one ax, three
bolos, the clothing on their backs plus one change of garments,
and several sleeping mats. This was the sum of their accumulated property after years of hard work as tenants. They had no
cooking utensils, no furniture, no carabao, and no cash savings.

Eusebio carefully organized the family's activities. Two of
the children went to school, the eldest two girls helped their
mother around the house, the younger ones ran errands and
helped their father with the simpler chores of farm work. After
a few months they built a house on the farm lot in order to be
close to their place of work and to be able to guard their harvest
against the raids of wild pigs.

Clearing and planting proceeded in stages. Only as much
land was cleared as could be planted and kept under cultivation. At the end of three years the Montanos had five of their
eight hectares cleared and cultivated. Two hectares were in
coffee interspersed with papayas and bananas to shade the
young coffee plants. Two hectares were planted with rice, and

after harvest this area was put into mongo beans and peanuts. The fifth hectare was devoted to ramie seedlings, corn, and fruit trees. When the remaining three hectares are cleared, they will be planted with rice as a temporary crop and at the same time with bamboo for construction purposes and coconuts as permanent crops.

After two years at EDCOR the Montanos were self-supporting. Eusebio said, "Our life here is better than it ever was on Luzon, and the best thing about it is that we own our land." The government had given him a house on this town lot, cooking utensils, a carabao, and rations until his crops were sufficient to support his family's needs. Summing up his account, Eusebio owes the government about ₱2,000. He expects to pay this amount without difficulty within a period of five years. His coffee plants, now shoulder high, already have fruit and will be ready for their first harvest this year. Figuring in the costs of harvesting and marketing and allowing for possible drops in prices, Eusebio can still count on an income of ₱4,000 a year from his two hectares in coffee alone. Add to this the cash income from rice, bananas, papayas, and ramie,* and the family food supply from vegetables, poultry, and pigs; and a yearly income of ₱10,000 becomes a realistic possibility for the EDCOR settlers once their farms are in full production.

The value of Eusebio's farm has greatly increased. According to the current price for uncleared forest land, his eight hectares were worth ₱240 at the time he began to develop his farm. When asked how much it was worth now, Eusebio pondered a minute and replied, "I wouldn't take ₱6,000 for it." To the ex-peasant who had never handled more than a few hundred pesos this amount was an ultimate for comparison. He was already tasting with relish the delightful independence of owning his own land.

Settler Garcia, an unmarried youth from the heart of Huklandia, shows what a single man and his brother can accomplish. Before he became a Huk he had farmed as a tenant on a fifty-fifty share arrangement. When he arrived at EDCOR in the spring of 1952 his sole possessions were the clothes he wore on his back. He had no tools, no utensils, no bedding, no work ani-

* Ramie is a fibrous plant from which very strong, durable cloth can be made.

mal, and no cash savings. The government gave him an ax, a bolo, a hoe, and a lot of advice and encouragement.

Garcia saw an opportunity to climb out of the depths of poverty. Carefully saving his ration of rice, he sold the surplus and bought a pressure kerosene lamp. During the day he cleared his land; in the cool of the night and by the light of his lamp he dug in the earth with his hoe. Evenings after school and on week ends, his brother helped. When Garcia obtained a carabao to do the heavy plowing, he believed his worst trials were over. Eighteen months after they arrived the Garcias became self-supporting. By the end of two years they had cleared six of their eight hectares.

This past season, in addition to a good rice harvest and supplementary crops of mongo beans, corn, and peanuts, Garcia tried a patch of watermelons. To his delight they did well, and he was able to sell ₱100 worth in the near-by market. This would provide spending money and school fees for his brother for a long time.

The Garcia account with EDCOR shows a debt of ₱1,600. In three more years he believes this debt can be entirely paid. At present he is self-supporting from the annual crops; next year his five hundred coffee trees will begin to bear. He has bananas ready to market. Ramie and avocados will begin to produce within a few years. He has good prospects of a handsome surplus over his own immediate needs as his farm comes into full production.

Not all the settlers have done this well, yet the total accomplishment is impressive. In two years, the settlers at Kapatagan cleared 495 hectares of virgin forest, an average of almost 5 hectares per settler. They harvested 3,159 cavans of palay* the first year and, in spite of a storm that ruined part of the crop, they took in 4,370 cavans the second season. In addition to the staple grain crop, the settlers supplemented their food supply with harvests of corn, mongo beans, and peanuts. Home gardens provided the families with an abundant supply of vegetables, bananas, and papayas after a few months of cultivation. Most of the settlers kept enough pigs and chickens to make a substantial addition to their diet.

* A cavan of palay is a large sack of unhusked rice weighing 44 kilos, or about 97 lbs.

The program of farm development was carefully planned and scheduled by the administration. The settlers were to devote the first month after their arrival to fencing and planting their home gardens. Next came the clearing of the farm lot, with the objective of two hectares cleared and planted to rice the first year. As soon as the rice was harvested, corn was to be planted, and before it was harvested the field was to be covered with peanuts or mongo beans. While the area was still under the cover crop the settler was to plant his permanent crops—abaca and bananas at Kapatagan, and coffee and ramie at Buldon. The second year, the cleared area would be enlarged, and so on until the entire farm was developed and the settler had become a prosperous farmer. By following this cycle of continuous planting and harvesting, the settlers gained experience in modern farm practice and learned to secure the maximum yield from the soil. Though some of the settlers were slow at first to appreciate this newer type of farming, by the end of the second year at Kapatagan most of them were converted. Walking across a field of freshly harvested palay, one could see the next crop already pushing its seed leaves through the soil.

According to the farm plan designed for Buldon, a settler should raise about ₱680 worth of rice and mongo beans the first year. The second year he should earn about ₱1,680 from his harvest of rice, mongo beans, ramie, and bananas. The third year his income should reach ₱3,280 with the addition of his first coffee crop. By the fourth year the settler should be self-supporting and no longer dependent upon the administration for help of any kind. In the long run the projected earning power of the Kapatagan farms is about the same as that for Buldon, since the cash value of abaca is about the same as that of coffee. As long as the market holds up, a farmer at Kapatagan with a good abaca crop might earn an income of as much as ₱10,000 a year. Though these figures may sound modest to those accustomed to incomes in the United States, they represent prospects far in excess of the average ₱400 yearly income of share tenants in the Philippines.[1] Indeed, an income of ₱10,000 a year in the Philippines would look enticing to college teachers and other professional groups whose incomes rarely exceed ₱6,000.

The best measure of the economic success of the EDCOR

farms is to be taken at Kapatagan, where more than two years of experience may be reviewed. Each year showed marked progress. After their first harvest at Kapatagan eight of the settlers found themselves so well off that they voluntarily gave up their ration. This impressed Defense Secretary Magsaysay so much that he wrote each a letter of congratulations, concluding, "I consider this splendid accomplishment on your part as the most sincere demonstration of your determination to live a peaceful and productive life." By September of 1953, 87 of the 100 settlers were getting along without rations. The farm administrator explained that about 20 of these 87 were still not totally supporting themselves from their farms but would make up the difference through odd jobs in the community. The other 13 settlers were living on what they produced on their land, supplemented by rations that had been reduced 50 per cent or more. Thus at the end of only two full years of effort, 67 out of the 100 settlers were living entirely off the produce of their own farms.[2] From the looks of crops at both projects in the spring of 1954, it appeared that many of the settlers would not only become self-supporting but also make substantial payments on their accounts.

Notable as these economic achievements are, the most impressive accomplishments have been in the social sphere. Most of the settlers' complaints still revolve around economic problems, while most of their enthusiasm for EDCOR stems from the democratic organizations that have flourished in the community. One of these is the public elementary school. Settlers who themselves never learned to read nor write speak with pride about sending their children to school. One of them, in his own forceful dialect, explained, "The EDCOR elementary school is established to save its peoples from educational blackout." And it was the settlers' own school! Officers of an active PTA were elected from among the ex-Huks. At Buldon this group organized a drive for funds to replace a leaky roof on the school building and to construct a unit for home-economics classes. Two months later they had raised nearly a hundred pesos.

Religion plays an important role in the life of the people. It lends grace and meaning to birth and death, and joy in the form of special celebrations and festival occasions. Most of the settlers are Catholics and worship in a chapel; the army has built one at each of the projects. Army chaplains serve as padres. They live among the people as one of them, sharing their food, their living arrangements, their sorrows, their pleasures. But the settlers exercise initiative and freedom even in the area of religion. Active Protestants among the settlers at Kapatagan are building their own chapel—not as a rival sect, but as their own contribution to the developing life of the community.

An ex-Huk at EDCOR said, "For the first time in my life, I have experienced a true democracy. The soldiers do not persecute us; they act as friends. If we have a complaint, we can go talk with the farm administrator. And we elect our own leaders to the town council." In a country where local government has long been weak, the creation of an elected town council at the EDCOR farms has been one of the most successful programs for the retraining of ex-Huks. Under the direction of the farm administrator and his staff, this council handles issues of concern to the community and receives training in preparation for the time when they will take complete responsibility for their affairs. The settlers think their local government is one of the best things about EDCOR. One of them wrote, "I was appointed as chief of police of this community. Disputes among the settlers and other minor cases were brought before me. Recently I was elected as a councilor to the Buldon settlers' government. My townmates [in my home province] were surprised how I came to such a position, because they thought that this place is for exile, not knowing that this is a portion of heaven." Another stated, "With democracy working full blast here in EDCOR you will find former transgressors of the laws of our land very peaceful citizens, more peace-loving than before. To ex-Huks, EDCOR is a place of rejuvenation."[3]

As the EDCOR settlements developed into flourishing communities the surrounding areas also grew and prospered. Within two weeks after the first EDCOR unit arrived at Kapatagan the price of chickens jumped from 80 centavos to ₱1.00, and finally stabilized at ₱1.50. Other products similarly have risen in value with the influx of the settlers and the greatly expanded local market. Sales in the leading Chinese store at Kapatagan jumped from ₱34,600 in 1951 to ₱791,477 in 1953. The operator of the launch from Ozamis City across the bay to the landing nearest Kapatagan tripled his service during this period. So convinced was he that the coming of EDCOR had made the difference that he insisted on transporting all army personnel free.

Municipal officials in Kapatagan were certain that EDCOR had brought prosperity to the community. Between 1951 and 1953 land-tax payments increased from ₱5,480 to ₱6,430. Business license fees jumped from ₱7,950 to ₱12,750. Residence certificates rose from ₱1,830 to ₱2,720. Although there had been no actual census since the founding of the EDCOR farms, the population increase in the adjacent areas has been dramatic. New settlers have crowded into the region to stake out a land claim or to develop an old one. School enrollment at Kapatagan indicates that these families in the area surrounding EDCOR far outnumber the EDCOR settlers themselves.[4]

The development of the farmlands outside the EDCOR boundaries is partly due to the new roads built by the army troops. Eleven kilometers of new highway were needed to connect the EDCOR townsite with the town of Kapatagan proper. Sixteen kilometers of streets were built within the townsite, and another twenty-four kilometers of farm roads facilitated travel from the outlying areas to the center of the community. Similarly, the establishment of the EDCOR farm at Buldon meant the construction of some twenty kilometers of streets and roads and the surfacing of additional kilometers of old roads to make them passable in all weather. What roads mean to a community may be seen in the development of bus service for passengers and produce. In the old days bus service was unknown; people hiked out of the jungle or pulled their produce to market on carabao sleds. Now the Kapatagan EDCOR Farm has eight buses a day from towns along the coast. Buldon enjoys a schedule of two round trips a day to and from the capital at Cotabato.

The presence of an army unit at EDCOR has also encouraged the development of the surrounding area. The soldiers provide the sense of security needed by the pioneers. As long as that security was missing the first pioneers in the Kapatagan plain neglected or abandoned their claims. With the coming of the army many of them returned and have remained to develop their farms. Even the Moro inhabitants near EDCOR have come to appreciate the presence of the army, for they realize the advantage of protection against marauding outlaw bands. Never before during their memory has the area been so free from cattle rustling and murder, never before so peaceful and prosperous. When Captain Jongko was asked about the future of the settlements, he replied, "The army will have to keep a unit here for about five years. After that the settlers can organize their own police force and take care of their own affairs."

EDCOR has been of service to the surrounding area in many other ways. Assistance in filling out applications for land titles is offered free of charge. Through its staff of officers EDCOR brings into the area technical know-how and agricultural expertness which is rare in the remote rural barrios of the Philippines. The EDCOR dispensary and medical service is primarily for the settlement, but all outsiders are given free first-aid treatment and free medical service. The patient is required to pay only for the medicines he needs whenever they are not available in the dispensary. This generous service to the larger community has won the support and gratitude even of the Moros, for whom medical care is a new experience. During the two-year period 1952–53, the doctor and nurse at the Buldon EDCOR farm clinic treated 6,046 patients, exclusive of army men and their families. At least half of these civilian patients came from outside the EDCOR boundaries.[5]

The contribution of the educational facilities is enormous. Where there had been only tall trees and a path through the jungle, EDCOR at Kapatagan now has a public elementary school with 14 teachers and 509 children. Some 330 of these are from nonsettler families. Two private high schools have recently opened classes in the community. Add to these facilities the reading center and adult education program, and EDCOR becomes the center of cultural activity in the area. Similarly at Buldon, the new elementary school, with 12 teachers and an enrollment of 407 students, brings education to this area for the first time. Almost one-third of the children in attendance come from families outside of EDCOR itself.[6] The chaplain keeps the library at the reading center, where pamphlets, magazines, and books are distributed.

In place of the usual dull existence endured by isolated pioneers, EDCOR has made possible recreational opportunities and stimulating contacts. Settlers and soldiers together at Buldon built a stage for local dramatic productions and talent programs. Electric lights make night meetings and entertainment possible. The church organizes celebrations of religious holidays; the whole community joins in an annual fiesta attended by people from miles around. A sports program is promoted through the school. Dances are homespun affairs in a hall with rough floors, but they are rollicking good fun. The EDCOR farms have created such a reputation for being enjoyable places to live that the army has more volunteers for this branch of the service than it can use.

The overwhelming majority of settlers at EDCOR want to stay there and make it their permanent home. Only 7 per cent of the ex-Huks at Kapatagan and at Buldon indicated that they would like to return to their home province if they had a good opportunity. Among the other 93 per cent, enthusiasm for EDCOR was phrased in simple and impressive language: "Even if the government paid my way back, I would stay only for a visit and return." "I have land here; I could not afford to leave." "Here I hope to get rich and educate my children." "On Luzon there is only trouble; here it is peaceful." Invariably, the ex-Huks were favorably impressed by the peaceful life at EDCOR. Their responses indicate that the side which can offer peace and security has a great advantage in winning the hearts of the people. The army at the EDCOR farms was doing just that.

CHAPTER NINE

HUK PROPAGANDA

After quietly collecting information for several months, twenty-two teams from the Military Intelligence Service and the Manila police staged simultaneous raids, in October 1950, on the suspected hideouts of Communist leaders in Manila. The roundup of the Politburo, the executive body of the Communist party, was surprising, devastating, and complete. It broke up the nerve center of the Communist movement and the source of direction and co-ordination of Huk activities. Among those captured was the General Secretary, José Lava, a lawyer who had conducted activities from his office on the Escolta in the heart of Manila and from his residence in the Mayflower Apartments.[1]

José Lava represents the intellectual leadership in the Huk movement. Well educated, refined, and deeply steeped in Marxist doctrine, he has been largely responsible for adapting the party line to local conditions in the Philippines. Wielding a facile and prolific pen, he has produced many articles and booklets which have shaped the course of the movement and which have been used as texts in the indoctrination schools for Huk recruits. Among them are:

"The Struggle Against Awaitism."
"Outline on Strategy and Tactics."
"Milestones in the History of the Communist Party in the Philippines."
"Twenty Years of Struggle of the Communist Party in the Philippines."
"Accounting for the People's Funds Received and Spent to Finance the Revolution."[2]

During the trial, in which Lava was sentenced to prison for life, he refused to defend himself but at the same time submitted to the court a forty-three-page "Memorandum on the Causes of and Solution to Dissidence in the Philippines." With noteworthy skill he traces the history of the Philippines from the 1896 revolution against Spain to the present time. His re-write of Philippine history is a reflection of the Communist party line. Rizal, the national hero, is pictured as a weak and ineffective reformist; Aguinaldo, who surrendered to the Americans, becomes a reactionary puppet; and Bonafacio, the man of violence, is portrayed as the real leader of the common man's revolt. Stating that this uprising had been thwarted by the adroit combination of American arms and diplomacy, he casts America in the role of the Big Bad Imperialist. The anti-American line is carried throughout his discussion of the events of recent years. He writes:

"It is therefore incontrovertibly clear that the present economic situation featured by import and exchange controls, inflation, scarcity of goods, growing unemployment, low wages and semi-starvation on the part of the great majority of the people composed of peasants and workers is directly traceable to the imperialist-feudal-comprador economy imposed by American imperialists upon our country, of which the Bell Trade Act is merely the inevitable culmination. As long as this pattern of our economy remains intact, so long will poverty continue in the midst of abundant human and natural resources. And as long as poverty continues, so long will it drive the exploited workers and peasants into dissidence and revolution to over-throw imperialist-feudal power and reorganize the economy to serve the interests of the exploited masses."[3]

Evaluating the prospects of completing the revolution that Bonifacio began, Lava points with assurance to international developments: "The people's revolution in China finally triumphed in 1949. United States imperialism is confused in Western Europe even while it is being battered in Korea and increasingly isolated in Asia. World imperialism has lost the initiative everywhere even while inter-imperialist contradictions are wrecking its unity. Under the developng situation there is no promise at all that the imperialist powers will regain the initiative from the rapidly rising forces of socialism and national liberation." Boasting that the Huk forces had greatly expanded in the Philippines, Lava also asserted, "The leadership of the Communist Party in the struggle for national liberation is now fully recognized."[4] This was his last comment before being sentenced. The court decision terminated his leadership in the armed revolt when it placed him in a cell behind the thick walls of the national prison at Muntinglupa.

In passing sentence on José Lava and his fellow intellectuals in the Politburo, Judge Castelo stated, "Notwithstanding your unfounded belief that your government is incompetent and beyond reform and that the only remaining recourse is to overthrow it, your government, on the other hand, has not lost hope in your chance to reform and relies on your Christian conscience and your ability and willingness to do it." The government has tried, but so far unsuccessfully, to win these men back to democracy. The prisoners are exposed to the influences of selected movies, a wide variety of literature, and lectures by the prison officials in charge of adult education. After three years of such treatment there are still no signs that Lava and the others like him have changed their minds. Another approach and more intensive efforts might bring results, but of necessity the effort must be conducted under the handicap of a prison environment which sharpens the resistance of the inmates to approaches by the administration. So far no effective approach to the die-hard Communists through argument or persuasion has been found.

Fortunately, the struggle for the minds of men is not confined to these few at the radical extreme. At the opposite pole among the revolutionists is a much larger group of poorly educated followers to whom Communist doctrine is only a vague body of principles. Their reasons for joining the Huks were many and varied, but they stayed and fought because they believed that a successful Huk revolt would bring them a better life. To win these individuals back to the government's side is not easy but is far from hopeless.

Take the case of Eduardo Española, one of the EDCOR settlers at Buldon. As far back as he could remember Eduardo had helped his father on the farm. They owned the land, but there was never time nor money for schooling. The war years came and passed, but still the young man followed the same monotonous routine of labor on the home farm. One day in 1950 a group of men came by his place and invited him to join the Huks. Among them was a former schoolteacher in his barrio; the others were strangers dressed and armed as soldiers. It seemed wiser to say "yes" than "no" to those in possesion of firearms. The poor people in the barrios could hardly do anything but acquiesce to the requests of armed men.

Eduardo was also impressed by the promises the Huks made. They offered him a job as cook at a salary of ₱100 a month. To Eduardo, who had never held this much money in his hands at one time before, this sounded like a big opportunity. He was promised free land later on and the chance to live a life of freedom. The Huks said nothing about fighting the government, and naïve Eduardo never thought to raise that all-important question.

As the weeks and months passed in the Huk camp, the new cook began to realize what he had gotten into: up early in the morning; work until late at night; pack hurriedly and flee and make camp in a new location; and always the dread fear of knowing he was hunted as an outlaw. This went on day after day, and nothing was ever said about the promised ₱100 a month wages. The prospects of obtaining land of his own seemed more remote than ever.

Then the Huk band that he was attached to began to break apart. A few were captured; the squadron commander deserted and surrendered. Fearful and discouraged, Eduardo gave himself up. In the army stockade he first learned about the EDCOR settlement in Mindanao. The opportunities described by the Civil Affairs officer sounded good to him, and he volunteered to go to Buldon.

EDCOR has meant a new life to Eduardo and to ex-Huks like him. The Communist doctrine, which had never been more than skin-deep, was soon forgotten in the excitement of clearing the jungle and developing a farm of his own. Encouraged by the kind treatment and stimulated by the opportunities around him, Eduardo is full of plans for his farm and his family at Buldon, where he intends to stay for the rest of his life. The problem of loyalty for this poor and ignorant ex-Huk vanished when he was given an opportunity to earn a decent living and become a self-respecting member of the community.

Even at the EDCOR farms, which exclude the ex-Huks with criminal charges against them or those deeply involved in the Communist conspiracy, there is a great variety among the settlers. Some, as in the case just cited above, had little or no indoctrination in Communist principles; others had received heavy injections of Marxist theory and had led in the expansionist drives of the Huks on Luzon and on Panay. The reasons for joining the Huks varied widely, as did the process whereby they established first contacts with the movement. Some joined the Huks because of the glowing promises in their propaganda, but others joined simply because of the circumstances and associations. Some aspects of the Huk propaganda appealed to one group, while different promises influenced others. To understand the propaganda war one must understand the background of wants and needs, of circumstances and association, of ideals and motives which characterize the Huks.

What kind of propaganda have the Huks used? They publish a newspaper called *Titis* (Flame); a magazine named *Kalayaan* (Freedom); and a constant stream of pamphlets, leaflets, and posters. Everything is mimeographed, and the text is usually illustrated with crudely drawn cartoons. The writing is a mixture of political analysis, comments on the news, stories of peasant exploitation at the hands of ruthless landlords, and appeals to support the National Liberation Movement, the Huks. All this is the work of a Communist organization known as PEIRA (Political, Economic, Intelligence, and Research Association), which collects the news, writes the articles, and designs the publications. This material then is widely distributed throughout the islands, but especially among the barrio people on Luzon.

The most obvious characteristic of the Huk propaganda is that it follows the party line of international communism. Hardly a single sheet of their literature since 1945 fails to rub salt into the sore of imperialism. The Huks have been vigorously and constantly anti-American. Much of the propaganda is devoted to international issues: the successful revolution in China, the Korean war, the "warmongering Americans." Filipinos were warned against participating in the Korean war, which was interpreted as a righteous effort on the part of Koreans to free themselves from the reactionary puppet, Syngman Rhee. The Huks advocate abolition of the military-bases agreement between the United States and the Philippines, claiming the presence of American troops endangers the peace of the Philippines. They bitterly oppose the presence of JUSMAG (Joint United States Military Advisory Group) which super-

vises the military aid given to the Philippines. Before the 1953
elections they tried to embarrass Magsaysay by referring to him
as "Jusmagsaysay."

Interestingly, this part of their propaganda barrage seems
to have had little effect even among the mass of their own followers. The interviews by the author with ex-Huks at EDCOR
revealed no evidence that they had been impressed by anti-
American ideas nor any other propaganda relating to international questions. The fact that they were being interviewed by
an American might presumably have inhibited a free expression of anti-American feeling; however, previous interviews
of the same individuals by Filipino officers and social workers
also failed to uncover any anti-American bias. In other interviews the author had discovered no reluctance to hold back
criticism of America. For example, he found that the top Huk
leaders among the Politburo confined in the National Prison
were completely free in their expression of anti-American ideas.
On the basis of these checks the credibility of the opinions obtained in the EDCOR interviews seemed justified. Also, other
facts support the conclusion that the anti-American campaign
has failed. Magsaysay, openly friendly with Americans, won
the last election on a larger majority in Pampanga Province, the
Huk stronghold, than he did in the nation at large. In spite of
all the Communist propaganda to the contrary, the friendship
between Filipinos and Americans seems to be closer since the
war than ever before.

In addition to the issues of imperialism and world politics,
the Huks have also emphasized local questions. They exploited
the chicanery involved in the 1949 elections to discredit the
government; during the 1953 campaign they denounced both
candidates in a pamphlet called "Quirino or Magsaysay." They
tried to stir up internal strife within the government in a pamphlet "Castelo vs. Duque, Who Is More Powerful?" Landlords
and moneylenders are constant targets and probably the butts of
their most effective propaganda. Many a poor man has found
the slogan, "Land for the landless, jobs for the jobless," hard to
resist.

Recognizing that the EDCOR settlements were a direct
threat to their own propaganda among the peasants, the Communists have gone to great lengths to counter the effect of this

army program. In a pamphlet devoted entirely to EDCOR, they pictured the EDCOR farms as concentration camps enclosed with barbed-wire fences, guarded by soldiers at sentry boxes, and inhabited by ex-Huks in chains. The Communist pamphlet stated that prisoners worked at the point of bayonets and had no time for rest. The whole project, they claimed, was an American idea to forestall a revolt against the weak and corrupt government.[5] This propaganda is pure and complete fabrication.

While the high command among the Huks was grinding out anti-EDCOR propaganda, the men in the ranks were covertly discussing the government offer. Ex-Huks at EDCOR reported a variety of reactions among their companions in the mountains before their surrender or capture. One said that most of the squadron commanders and men in the ranks believed the good reports about EDCOR, and that the top brass also believed it but could not afford to say so. Some of the Huk leaders in statements to their men said that EDCOR was mere propaganda; others took the line that it was temporary and would collapse in failure as soon as Magsaysay turned his attention elsewhere. Some of the Huks talked about EDCOR secretly for fear that they would be shot for discussing the possibility of surrender. One of the Huks said that the men in his unit had been "disgusted with EDCOR, because they believed it was only a lure to get them to surrender." But another stated that all of his comrades wanted to surrender in order to take advantage of the free land offered at EDCOR. The official party lecturers admonished the Huks not to believe the propaganda about EDCOR: "Once there, you will be liquidated." A variation of this same idea was the threat, "EDCOR may look good at the moment; but when the army withdraws after some time, the Moros will then murder everyone." Some of the Huks said that they did not believe the constructive program of EDCOR was true because the army was killing so many Huks in the military action in Luzon. Officially, the Huk policy toward EDCOR is clear. They denounce it as a trick to get Huks to surrender, and any indication of intention to surrender is sufficient cause for liquidation. Many ex-Huks testified to the actuality of this threat.[6] The Huk units in the field varied widely in their reaction to the EDCOR program; to many, EDCOR sounded too good to be true.

The army's resettlement program immediately revealed the real purpose behind the Huk appeal of "land for the landless." When the army started giving land to the landless, the Huks tried to sabotage the effort. Their agents tried to wreck the Kapatagan project; their gunmen ambushed the EDCOR engineers on their way to the new farm in Isabela Province. The Huks are not primarily concerned with agrarian reform. Like their Communist cousins before them in China and Russia, agrarian reform is a convenient issue to secure a popular support and justify seizing power. The Huks saw EDCOR as a threat to their major propaganda weapon, and they did not take the threat lightly.

In the course of interviewing the ex-Huks at the EDCOR farms, the author asked them to state what was the most attractive part of the Huk appeal. "What part of their program, or which of their promises, did you like best?" Out of 108 answers, 23 said that they did not like anything about the Huk propaganda nor the Huk organization. These were the individuals who had been forced to join the movement. The statements by the other 85 may be divided into three classifications: first, all those who mentioned land distribution to the peasants; second, the ones chiefly impressed by the Huks as champions of the oppressed and the advocates of equality; and third, those who liked having firearms, the discipline in the Huk units, the fight against the corruption in government, and other miscellaneous items.

The most impressive single item of Huk propaganda is "land for the landless." Some 54 per cent of the ex-Huks interviewed testified that this promise was either a major cause of aligning themselves with the movement or a factor in strengthening their loyalty to the Huks. To men who had always lived on the land and always earned their livelihood from the soil, and who year after year had measured the difference between poverty and well-being by the share of the harvest taken by the landlord, the prospect of owning land made a strong appeal. This agrarian appeal, however, was often coupled with other promises and programs. To many of them "jobs for the jobless" was equally attractive. Others were impressed by the Huk promises of free schools and free medical care. In the minds of most of the Huks who were attracted by the promises of agrarian reform was a desire for justice, which meant equality of treatment in the courts and the abolition of usury.

This leads to the next largest group, 28 per cent of the total, for whom the Huks had become the champions of the poor and the down-trodden masses. Those in this group were attracted by the Huks' sympathy for the oppressed. The Communists craftily exploited the strong emotional identification of idealistic individuals with a class which they believed had been treated unfairly. The Huks, by casting themselves in the role of righteous protectors, made a strong appeal for the allegiance of persons with a highly developed sympathy for the dispossessed. Such individuals are always fair game for a revolutionary group advocating a theory of class warfare.

Those in the third category were attracted mostly by strong features of the Huk organization. One said that he liked the close-knit unity and discipline of his squadron. Another stated that he was greatly impressed by the philosophical basis of the Communist theory, which made it possible to explain events and provide answers to problems. Several were interested primarily in the opportunity to carry firearms. Theirs was a clear case of adolescent desire for power in which firearms as symbols of authority were identified with social position, the basic ingredient in power. Others liked the Huks because they opposed the Japanese invaders during the war, or because more recently they had advocated cleaning up the government and establishing a "new democracy." Stripped of all its trappings this "new democracy" was simply the old Marxist idea of the dictatorship of the proletariat, but a skunk by some other name will always fool a few.

The above analysis of Huk propaganda shows what appealed to the members and what did not, but the question of motives for joining the movement is largely left untouched. Many of the Huks did not join because of an idea or doctrine. The indoctrination usually came later, after they had already become active Huks. Only among the intellectuals and top leaders of the Communist party is the doctrinal aspect of the movement a first and paramount attraction. In the ranks and among the mass of followers the bread-and-butter promises, fear of the Constabulary, coercion by the Huks, and accidental association were the primary moving forces.

CHAPTER TEN

THE STRUGGLE FOR THE MINDS OF MEN

Why did 100,000 Filipinos at one time become active members or sympathetic supporters of the Huks? What motives and processes led them into the movement? These questions can best be answered by examining a representative group of individuals who have been active Huks. The author was able to study intensively the experiences of 95 ex-Huks at EDCOR, who were selected at random so as to include the wide range from well-educated leaders to illiterate followers. This EDCOR group represents all the major types of experience among the Huks with the exception of the hard core of intellectual leaders, and probably gives a good picture of the relative importance of the different sources of motivation.

Well over half the ex-Huks had become members without being moved to any appreciable degree by ideas.[1] Only 14 cases were found where verbal persuasion, or propaganda, was the sole motivating force in their joining the revolution. Among these, 10 were interested chiefly in agrarian issues, such as land distribution and the abolition of usury, or equality and help for the oppressed. In another 26 cases, persuasion was a contributing influence in a complex of motives. For example, effective Communist teaching prepared Alfredo Cruz for membership in the Huks. In 1945 he joined a youth organization in his barrio, which Communists had heavily infiltrated. He already knew what it meant to be poor, but he learned in the youth organization about a "new democracy" which could be gained by fighting oppression. In order to stop exploitation, the poor must organize and fight for their rights. Believing these ideas, Alfredo joined other youths in supplying food to the Huks. When they were discovered by the army he fled from his barrio and joined a fighting squadron in the mountains. Later he became chairman of a section organizing committee, where he had an opportunity to exercise his interest in ideas.

Vicente Cuevas represents those whose motives in joining the Huks were a mixture of propaganda and circumstances. A natural leader in his barrio, Vicente became the local contact man

116

for the Huk field command in that area. He helped to arrange a Huk rally, which was attended by all the townspeople. In their enthusiasm they decided to form their own Huk unit, and Vicente became its head by popular decision. He could hardly refuse without arousing suspicion, and he could not afford to run away from his family and his tailoring business. Propelled into the movement by the sweep of these events, he then attended a Stalin university, where he took short intensive courses on Marx, Lenin, Stalin, Lincoln and Jefferson (carefully edited and selected), the state, military tactics, democracy (Russian style), and revolution. He absorbed much of the Communist doctrine and became an advocate of the party propaganda. He believed that the present Philippine government was corrupt and should be changed, that land should be distributed to the peasants, and that usury should be abolished. One of the Communists' strongest points, he thought, was the fight for justice against the landlords. Following the doctrine that labor and not capital is the source of progress, Vicente advocated a larger share of profits for workers. Thoroughly involved in revolutionary activity; he was expecting a promotion in the Huk hierarchy when he was captured in March 1951.

In spite of the popular notion that the Huks are mostly bandits and social misfits, there is little evidence from a study of Huk personnel to support such opinion. On the contrary, the Huks maintain a strict moral code and have expelled some members and liquidated others for acts of crime.[2] The lawlessness of the Huks is of a political nature: crimes against the state, or acts of violence in the course of revolution. These may more easily excuse an individual Communist from a sense of personal guilt; nevertheless, they are more serious than ordinary low-class burglary and murder. Likewise, there is little evidence that the Huk movement is an escape for persons with unsolved personal problems. In only four cases among those studied at EDCOR could the motive for joining the Huks be classified as personal, and in these few cases the difficulty could be accurately described as idleness, curiosity, or restlessness—hardly appropriate ills to be described as maladjustment. In the great majority of cases the motives were social; that is, they were appeals to companionship by close friends or relatives, or they were promises based on the mistreatment of the Japanese during the occupation, the malfunctioning of the government, the miscarriage of justice, or the abuses of a tenant system.

No single motive, not even the agrarian issue, accounts for more than a small minority of those who joined the Huks. If any group of Huks would be likely to count agrarian problems high among reasons for joining the revolution, it should be those at EDCOR, who were interested in land and who volunteered to come to Mindanao. Yet in only ten cases was the desire for land, or the plight of the poor tenant, or some similar phrasing of agrarian unrest solely responsible for their joining the Huks. For another eighteen individuals, agrarian complaints were an important item among a complex of several motives. Together these constitute only 29 per cent of the ex-Huks at EDCOR. One is forced to realize that the agrarian issue is only one of a number of talking points for the Communists and that propaganda itself, though important, is not the chief means of adding new recruits. Once in the fold, a new member was often so impressed by the promises of land distribution that he stayed on as a loyal Huk. Even more important than its usefulness as a recruiting issue and as a subject of indoctrination, the agrarian problem is adroitly handled by the Communists to give the revolutionary conspiracy a righteous and high-sounding tone.

Huk leaders have long realized that recruiting could not wait for the slow process of persuasion and free decision. Among ex-Huks interviewed at EDCOR, nineteen had been forced to join at the point of a gun or because of threats of violence against their families. In another twelve cases the use of force was an important element among several related factors. Thus, among the ex-Huks at EDCOR force had been used as a recruiting procedure in more instances than the appeal of agrarian reform.

The experience of young Felix Tanduay shows how pressure was applied to families to force individuals to join the Huks. During the expansion of the Huk activities on the island of Panay, Huk commander Capadocia ordered each of several barrios to send three bright, promising girls to the Stalin University, which had been established in the mountains. The leader of the Huks in Felix's home barrio picked the sister of Felix as one of the new recruits. The Tanduay family was

The old and the young join in threshing the grain by foot.

Settlers harvest the first rice crop at Kapatagan.

Winnowing, drying, and sacking are usually the work of women.

Settlers carry the grain from their farm lots to the townsite over roads that are quagmires in the rainy season.

The Queen of the Harvest leads a parade during the festival celebrating the first harvest at Kapatagan.

The farm administrator (*center*) and the mayor (*to his right*) meet with members of the town council at Buldon EDCOR Farm.

A former Huk commander is now the industrious mayor of Buldon EDCOR Farm.

Settlers and soldiers put spirit into a game of volleyball.

It is community playtime on the grounds in front of the school at Kapatagan.

Settlers at Kapatagan EDCOR Farm attend regular services at an attractive church.

The EDCOR communities maintain piggeries and encourage the raising of good stock.

Settlers and soldiers together build a stage for movies and home-talent shows.

Settlers and their families are engrossed in the feature attraction at a home-talent show.

Children of ex-Huks at Kapatagan: "I pledge allegiance to the Republic of the Philippines . . ."

The army doctor and nurse extend free medical care to settlers
and also to civilians living near EDCOR.

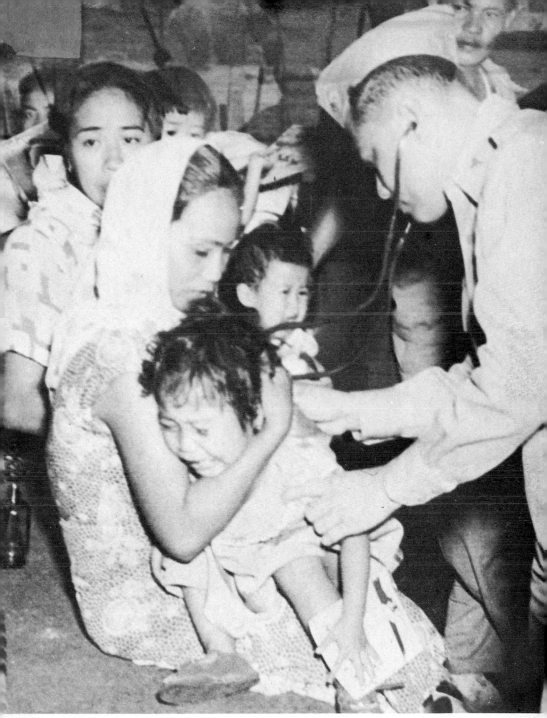

The army doctor holds a clinic for the children of the settlers.

The author interrupted a settler at work on his abaca farm at Kapatagan. When fully developed, the farm could yield an income of 10,000 pesos a year.

An abaca stripping machine, operated co-operatively, helps the EDCOR settlers at Kapatagan to prepare hemp for market at a minimum cost and labor.

Two hundred were expected, but two thousand came to the opening ceremonies of the third EDCOR settlement in Isabela Province.

The winding street, attractive cottages, and running water impress visitors to the new EDCOR settlement.

Major V. O. Valenova brings official army greetings to the Moro Sultan, whose co-operation has made it possible to establish a fourth EDCOR settlement in Cotabato Province.

Luis Taruc surrenders to Major General Jesus Vargas (*center*) in the presence of army aides and Under-Secretary of Defense José Crisol (*left*).

Luis Taruc, in confinement, awaits trial after his surrender.

deeply troubled. They dared not say no, because several people in near-by places had been killed for refusing to obey the Huk demands. While the family was debating what to do, Felix returned home from the town where he had been attending high school as a boarding student. When he saw his sister in tears and learned about the Huk order, he volunteered to go to the mountains in her place. Though it meant the interruption of his schooling, the family agreed to this substitute arrangement, since no other good alternative seemed available. In this manner the Huks obtained a youth who served their cause loyally, if not voluntarily, in order to protect his family.

Sometimes individuals joined the Huks to avoid further persecution or terrorism by the government forces. This was true of 19 per cent of the ex-Huks at EDCOR. One might say that they were shoved into the arms of the revolutionaries by the very efforts of the army to suppress the armed revolt. For example, in 1946, during the effort to stamp out the dissident movement by force, Francisco Dalmar was captured by the civilian guards. Suspecting that he was a Huk, they beat him and kicked him but finally turned him loose when he refused to confess. Embittered and determined to seek revenge, he decided to join a Huk unit. Heading toward the mountains, he soon met a squadron commander, who inducted him into the organization. After two weeks under observation he received a gun and became an active Huk.

Sometimes soldiers who had been active guerrillas during the war joined the Huks in anger against the government for depriving them of their back pay. This was true of the experience of 8 per cent of the ex-Huks at EDCOR. Many a loyal guerrilla fighter, for example, suffered the same disappointment as Antonio Sarangaya. During the period of the Japanese occupation he fought with a USAFFE unit recognized by the United States Army. When the time came for mustering out after the fighting was over in 1945, all the men in his organization applied for back pay. One after another his companions received a fat check for services rendered to Uncle Sam, but nothing came for Antonio. Finally one day an officer from the Finance Division approached him and suggested that for a certain "fee" he could arrange the back pay. When Sarangaya complained that he was broke, the officer tore up his application papers in his presence. In disgust and anger Antonio joined the Huks, "determined to die if necessary in order to clean up the government." The program of back pay to the veterans of the guerrilla campaigns, though well intentioned, damaged the reputation of the government because of its corrupt administration.

Among 8 per cent of the ex-Huks at EDCOR the chief motive in joining the dissident cause was a sense of personal obligation to former friends. This strong bond is rooted in Philippine society and especially in the family, where it is almost impossible to say "no" to the request of a friend or relative. Strange as this may sound to Western man, who is accustomed to a more loosely knit social system, the feeling of obligation to accede to the request of a friend is still a powerful motive in the Orient. Communism makes use of this custom in recruiting followers; then, if the events of recent years in China are indicative, it ruthlessly destroys the familial bonds as a threat to the totalitarian state.

An interesting example of the power of this sense of obligation to friends is found in the experience of Nicanor Hernandez. He first joined the Huks early in the war in 1942 because he "believed in their cause." During the fighting for liberation in 1945 he contracted malaria and went home to recover. By the time he was well the war had ended. Believing that his days with the Huks were over, Hernandez married a neighborhood sweetheart and settled down to farming. But next year the Huks were reactivated and many of his former companions joined. Hernandez did not wish to leave his new wife and the peace of home. But his friends asked him to come, and he went with them. He explained, "I could not say no. I was one of them, and I felt that this was my obligation."

Why they joined the Huks is inseparable from the process of how they joined, for motivation includes the entire complex of action in becoming a Huk and not simply the reasons which one may give for joining or the appealing aspects of the Huk propaganda. Becoming a Huk is a series of interlocking acts, one leading to another like links in a chain. Usually, first contact with the movement came through force, or accident, or friendly associations. Intellectual assent and indoctrination ordinarily followed later. This sequence was not invariable, but it was characteristic of the experience of most of the Huks studied.

Two examples from among the EDCOR settlers illustrate the order of events which gradually involved them in the Huk movement and finally led to a mental reorientation, or conversion to the "party line." Cecilio Lepanto, a young man, helped his father farm on a place far from town. One day the Huks passed his house and asked him to help carry supplies. The request was polite; and also, since the men were armed, he felt that he had to go. He was not reluctant, since some of the Huks had been his friends. Later, when they were in the mountains, the Huks told Lepanto that he had better stay with them because the Constabulary would learn that he had helped the Huks and would persecute him. In the days that followed the Huks explained their program. When the revolution succeeded, they said, Lepanto and other farmers would receive free land. Those now living in poverty would have jobs and privileges. He believed these promises and stayed in the mountains to become an active Huk. What began as innocent association led finally to voluntary service undergirded by political conviction.

Victor Benedicto has a forceful personality and an education which elevates him above the man in the ranks. During the war he fought in a guerrilla band on Luzon, but in the political juggling afterward his outfit failed to receive recognition and back pay. He took a job as bus driver in Laguna Province. One day his bus was stopped by a Huk squadron, and Benedicto was kidnaped and taken to their camp. Although he was kept a captive, he was treated kindly and fed a constant diet of Huk propaganda. Recalling the experience, he said, "I was convinced of the good intentions of the Huks: their defiance of crooked government officials, their fight for justice, and their hard work. I was pleased with what I saw and heard, so I joined them." First he was captured, then he decided to join. Intellectual conviction is not less important because it comes after overt action, for the staunch doctrinal core of communism gives the revolution its staying power. Individuals may have drifted casually into the movement or may have been forced to join, but they remain and endure the rigors of guerrilla life because of a belief that only communism will bring about justice and equality and the good life to the masses.

Assuming that the initial link between an individual and the Huks is an important point in the life cycle of a revolutionary, the author asked the ex-Huks at EDCOR to tell about their first contact with the movement. Here are the results: the largest number, about 38 per cent, became involved in the Huks through personal friendship. Some 20 per cent were "invited" to join by armed strangers; while almost an equal number, some 18 per cent, were kidnaped or captured. About 11 per cent of the individuals sought out the Huks voluntarily. Smaller numbers entered the movement through feeder organizations, or through the influence of someone in authority, or upon the invitation of unarmed Huk organizers.

Against this background of varied motives, desires, interests, and experience on the part of the Huks, the government's efforts to recapture the loyalty of its wayward citizens can be better appreciated. Having traced the process whereby one becomes a Huk, what is the reverse pattern of restoring him to normal society and rehabilitating him for democratic citizenship? The Huks rely largely upon force to fill their requirements for new recruits; the army likewise uses force to recapture them. Force employed by both sides accounts for the largest single shift in manpower, but force alone can no more explain the strength of the government's appeal to the loyalty of its citizens than it can account for the popularity of the Huks among thousands of Filipinos. Clues to the subtler factors which incline men toward democratic government and away from communism come not from those Huks captured in military action but from those who escaped from their squadrons and surrendered voluntarily to the government.

Among the ex-Huks interviewed at the EDCOR farms were sixty who had surrendered. Each of them was asked to explain why and how this had happened. Often several factors were involved in any single surrender, as was true of motivation for joining the Huks. However, the reasons given for surrender fall neatly into four groups: first, the hardships of life in the mountains; second, the failures and disappointments of the Huk organization; third, opportunities offered by the government; and fourth, family pressures to surrender.

The life of the Huk guerrilla in the Philippines is more difficult in many respects than that of his brother Communist in China, North Korea, or Indochina. The difference is largely one of geography. In those countries the Communists have been able to fight a territorial war and to defend land areas which could be developed as bases of operations. In the small and rugged island world of the Philippines such a territorial sanctuary for the Huks has never been possible. The army occupies the inhabited areas in the lowlands and periodically sends expeditions into the mountains to destroy Huk hideouts. This leaves the guerrillas only one recourse, a furtive and mobile existence. Some 61 per cent of those who surrendered cited hardships in the mountains as the chief factor in their decision to give up. One after another they registered complaints against exposure to the cold, the lack of food, and the loss of sleep. Many of these difficulties resulted from the frequent attacks of the armed forces. After two to six years of guerrilla existence many of the ex-Huks said, "I was tired of a fugitive life; all I wanted was to live peacefully."

The next most important factor, which was cited by 45 per cent of those who surrendered, was related to Huk failures. Some reacted to the strict Huk discipline and to the fact that they were forced to obey distasteful orders. They explained that the revolution was not progressing and would end in failure. Loss of hope in victory destroyed morale and led to discouragement and surrender. After months and months of effort and no returns, some of the Huks began to believe that the promises of their leaders were lies. In some instances the leader had surrendered with his men; in others, where the leader had been killed, the men decided to give up.

Some 23 per cent of those surrendering were attracted to the government's side by various promises and opportunities. The one most often cited was the offer of free land, but almost as frequently mentioned was the promise that those who surrendered would not be tortured. Some were attracted by an offer of a job, a few by the practice of paying for surrendered firearms, and others by the generous policy of freeing those with no criminal charges against them.

Only twenty-seven out of the sixty surrendered Huks had heard of EDCOR before their decision to give themselves up.

However, all but nine of those who had been informed about the new army program were wholly or partly influenced to surrender by it. The following statements indicate the impression made:

"News of EDCOR gave us hope for a new life."

"It greatly influenced my surrender, and I planned to volunteer to go to Mindanao."

Many said, "The promise of land and help by EDCOR was an important factor in my surrender."

"We decided to surrender only after we heard about EDCOR."

Several said, "I read the leaflets about EDCOR, which had been dropped by planes, and decided to surrender."

"I was already thinking about surrendering; EDCOR clinched my decision."

"When my parents and brother told me about EDCOR, I believed them and surrendered."

"We reasoned that life at EDCOR would be much better than fighting with the Huks; so we surrendered and applied to go to one of the settlements."

A small number, only 5 per cent, had surrendered because of family pressures. This took several forms. In a few instances, during the period when the writ of habeas corpus was suspended, the armed forces held family members as hostages on charges of conniving with the Huks. More often, the relatives urged the individual in the Huks to surrender. Sometimes he was needed at home to earn a living for his family. These pressures would undoubtedly be more important were it not that most of the Huks are unmarried youths with little family responsibility.

The fact that surrendered or captured Huks move physically from one side to the other is important but does not necessarily mean that a corresponding mental reorientation has taken place. One who is tired of the hard, dreary life in the mountains may surrender but still believe that the Huks have the right ideas. Realizing this, the government has carried on a vast program of education for democracy. Among the population at large this has been the task of the public schools, the adult education programs, and special campaigns organized by the Civil Affairs officers. EDCOR has undertaken the more difficult job of reorienting the ex-Huks. This has been vastly different from "brain washing." The approach, itself democratic, has been to place the ex-Huks in a community of their own, but not isolated from the world around them, to give them maximum freedom and opportunity, and to encourage them to develop into responsible and loyal citizens. How successful this has been may be seen from the settlers' own responses to the program.

What do settlers like most about the EDCOR farms in Mindanao? What has impressed them most and influenced them to become pro-government in their sympathies? In his interviews with the settlers the author asked these questions: What do you think of life at EDCOR? Have you written letters to your family or friends? What did you tell them about EDCOR? Do you have any complaints or problems? What are your plans for the future?[9] The answers to these questions revealed in all but six cases one or more points of positive and favorable response to the life at the farms.

As would be expected, the largest number of settlers, about 58 per cent, were impressed by government aid in the form of housing, a home lot, a ration of food, and farm equipment. Almost as large a number, some 51 per cent, mentioned the free land. When asked what they thought of life at EDCOR, the settlers' faces would light up as they replied, "Here we have land!" One of them wrote in a letter to his brother, "I have a good farm lot. The children are growing stout here and are not sickly as they were in Manila." The brother replied, "You are better off than I am, because you have a piece of land." One whose face was permanently wrinkled by the hardships and worry during his years with the Huks said, "I am luckier than one who wins first prize in the sweepstakes, because here I have land that cannot be stolen. I could never own land in Luzon. I am comfortably settled in the most peaceful place in Mindanao, and I want to stay here a lifetime."

As many as 41 per cent of the settlers were impressed by the fact that it was peaceful at EDCOR. Taken for granted by the ordinary citizen, peace became the pearl of great price to these Huks who had not possessed it in many years. The people in Huklandia had lived so long in the shadow of war that they turned in gratitude to the government which provided the basic conditions for a happy life. The turbulent experience of Carlos Barbero is typical of many others. He joined the Huks in 1942 during the early days of the Japanese occupation. At the end of fighting in 1945, Carlos went home to his farm, but in a few months he was called back to his Huk unit by his former companions. Next year during the discussion of amnesty he slipped quietly back to his farm, where he led an uncertain civilian existence until 1951. In that year a Huk raid in a near-by barrio led to a Constabulary roundup of all suspects in the area. Carlos Barbero was among them. While in the stockade, he was beaten and punished severely. To him EDCOR was at first a welcome relief from prison. Once he was settled at the farm, it became an answer to his dreams. He said, "I like it here very much. It is peaceful. If one works hard, there is plenty of food. The past is over, and I will forget it. EDCOR is a wise program, which is helping poor people. The great advantage here is the peaceful condition."

Some of the ex-Huks look back upon their life in Luzon as a nightmare. One expressed the idea simply, "I prefer it here to Luzon because it is safer. We only have the Moros to deal with here. On Luzon, former companions in the Huks will shoot you; and if they don't, enemies in the civil guard will." Another, who had escaped from his Huk squadron in order to surrender, said, "There is a future here. It is peaceful. I would not dare return to my native province in Luzon."

Some 35 per cent of the settlers were impressed by the opportunities at the EDCOR farms. Their comments ran like this one: "Life here is excellent compared with that on Luzon. The land is very rich. With work and proper care it yields a big harvest. We have a chance to become prosperous. I am free. What I put into my land is mine." Sometimes, in the settler's enthusiasm he exaggerated the truth. One wrote to his father and mother, "The situation here is very good; one can easily get rich." One could not really get rich on an eight-hectare farm, but the sudden gift of opportunities to those who had never had any was enough to excite the imagination.

In 24 per cent of those interviewed, the good treatment by the army and the pleasant conditions of life influenced the settlers in developing pro-government attitudes. For example,

Juan Cunanan, who was a member of a peasant organization, the PKM, and who gave occasional aid to the Huks, was picked up by the army in 1951 and charged as a Huk agent. When he refused to confess, he was beaten and hit with the butt of a gun. He came to EDCOR with bitterness in his heart toward the armed forces. Two years later he said, "I like it here. I have forgotten all the harm done because of the good treatment. I have only brotherly love toward the people here."

Salvador Moreno had also been a member of the peasant organization which supplied the Huk army. Weary of the heavy work of gathering food supplies, he tried to escape from the clutches of the Huks, only to run into an army patrol which took him to the stockade. A surrendered Huk pointed to him as a Huk member. Refusing to confess, he was beaten until he lost consciousness. This was repeated seven times until he finally "confessed" to save himself. When interviewed, Moreno said, "I must admit that I came to EDCOR without much hope of good treatment by the army. Since then, I have had to change my mind. I realize now that it was not the fault of the army but of the surrendered Huk who gave them false information. I am willing to forget the past. All my hopes are here in my farm."

Domingo Alvarez was captured in 1951. For years he had fought with a guerrilla unit, believing that "loyalty to country meant loyalty to the Huks." After his first year at EDCOR he wrote to his father about "the good treatment by the government and his house and the lot and farm." In reply the father wrote, "I know this cannot be true, but behave in the stockade where you are so that you will not be punished." Domingo had to send his parents a picture of himself and his family in front of their house in order to convince them that EDCOR was real. A year of good treatment was enough to change Domingo from his former allegiance to the Huks.

To many, the good treatment at EDCOR was related to free public schools for the children, medical care, and the opportunity for settlers to take a hand in their own affairs. One settler said, "I would not return to Luzon for a thousand pesos; I would not even go on a visit. We have a real democracy in living here." Another, who had been beaten nearly to death in a stockade, said, "Before I came here I disliked the government; now I have experienced a true democracy. I like it here very much." An ex-Huk, who had spent four months in confinement before coming to EDCOR, said, "This is a place where democracy is practiced in full swing. The government gives material aid to every settler and encourages them in their work by giving them every opportunity to make good and start life anew."

The EDCOR program is actually restoring faith in the government among men who have been active Communists. Although the effort involves only a few hundred individuals, the record is impressive. The government has not been slow to use this experience in the larger struggle for the minds of men. One issue of "Troop Information," an armed-forces mimeographed pamphlet for troop education, was devoted entirely to EDCOR. All soldiers were urged to study what the army was doing to rehabilitate ex-Huks and be able to explain the project to any who might inquire. Civil Affairs officers distributed picture posters and bulletins on EDCOR in all towns and barrios of the land. Army planes dropped EDCOR leaflets over Huk-infested areas. Mobile units of the United States Information Service showed movies of EDCOR and conducted public discussions featuring these projects in most of the towns of the islands. A USIS picture pamphlet, "The Philippines Solves Its Communist Problem," was devoted exclusively to EDCOR. It was circulated by the thousands throughout the Philippines and abroad. Foreign journalists hurried to the EDCOR farms to see for themselves, and soon articles on the new approach to the Communist problem appeared in the popular magazines of America. The publicity about EDCOR received major support when a Philippine movie company, LVN, turned out a well-produced film in the Tagalog dialect, entitled "Huk," which featured the new life of the former dissidents at EDCOR. A version of the film in English carried enough interest to play in the theaters of America.

All of this publicity had a double purpose: It was beamed toward the Huks in hopes that an increasing number of them would surrender; and it was directed to the wider public in the perennial effort to build confidence in democracy. The results are clear. The old army of persecution became "the army with a social conscience"; the government of the landed aristocracy became the government concerned with the welfare of the people; and the man who fathered EDCOR, Ramon Magsaysay, became the next president of the Republic of the Philippines.

CHAPTER ELEVEN

TOWARD VICTORY

On the morning of May 17, 1954, Luis Taruc, the most popular Huk leader among the peasants of Central Luzon, "gave up." He preferred to avoid the term surrender, and the government humored his feelings by agreeing to other words meaning the same thing. Taruc, the head of the Huk guerrilla forces against the Japanese during World War II and an important member of the Communist Politburo, the party's top policy-making body, was at last in government hands. He had sent word to a *Manila Times* news reporter, Benigno Aquino, that he accepted the government terms and would give up. Aquino, who for months had tried to negotiate a surrender of Huk forces, drove his car down a dusty barrio road toward the meeting place. He had to pass through Philippine Army troops, who maintained heavy patrols around the area. Several kilometers farther at the side of the road Taruc stood ready and waiting. He was alone except for some of the older people of the barrio. The heavily armed elite guards so evident at past meetings were absent. With little conversation except the words, "I accept," Taruc entered the car with Aquino and sped back down the road. At the army outpost they were joined by an intelligence officer who provided safe conduct to army headquarters near Manila. Within an hour Taruc had been turned over to the doctors for a medical checkup prior to confinement.

Newsmen were permitted to take pictures but not to interview the captive. The government had learned through past experience that Taruc was a master at using news releases for propaganda purposes. Neither would the government be party to publicity that might promote sympathy for Taruc as a folk hero. The administration immediately stopped all talk of a general amnesty for the Huks by stating that Taruc would not be granted a reprieve and that he would have to stand trial. By the end of the week the government lawyers had prepared the charges, twenty-six of them, a conviction on any one of which might lead to a death sentence or life imprisonment. The case was ready for the courts. These were the fast-moving events during the third week of May 1954. To explain their occurrence and interpret their meaning requires an understanding of events that started five months earlier.

After the new Magsaysay administration came into office in January 1954, the Huks tried to negotiate an amnesty which would permit them to come down out of the hills and operate peacefully as a legalized Communist party. Taruc stated that he would be willing to help in Magsaysay's program of barrio improvement by organizing peasants. In his effort to create sympathy and obtain freedom he offered his services without salary. The government of course refused to snap at this bait. The infiltration and sabotage from within could be much worse than the armed struggle in the field. After several weeks of fruitless discussion of surrender terms the deadline set by the government passed, and the army launched vigorous and sustained drives to capture the dissidents. The Huks were chased from mountains to swamps and from one hideout to another. They were on the run. Every few days some were killed in skirmishes; others were captured or surrendered and were added to the growing numbers in army stockades.

The friendly and considerate treatment of the civilians by the army won their co-operation and greatly improved the army intelligence network. Every time the Huks moved, someone would tip off the army, which followed hot on the heels of the fleeing dissidents. In one month Taruc lost several members of his elite guard and many of his trusted followers, including the chief of his supply division. All of them were captured by the army. At the time he gave up, Taruc's forces were reduced to a handful of weary, battered, and disorganized men. The day before, the army patrols had been to the very house where Taruc was in hiding. He had narrowly escaped capture on that occasion. The army had surrounded the area and was crosscrossing it with patrols day and night. The cordon tightened. Taruc probably chose to surrender as the only alternative to save his skin; he has not indicated that he gave up because he had a change of heart. In a court trial he could rely upon a winsome tongue to talk his way out of the electric chair and ultimately perhaps to freedom.

There are other incidents that must be considered in connection with Taruc's surrender. Several months previously the army had intercepted some correspondence between Communist leaders which reported that Taruc had been reprimanded by the party for failure to carry out orders and that he had been dismissed from the Politburo. In the same correspondence Taruc's brother, Peregrino, was reported as expelled from the party for not clearing propaganda releases with the Secretariat, a three-man executive body. The correspondence had some of the earmarks of authenticity, but the circumstances of its capture on the person of a common Huk courier led to suspicions that it might be a "plant." The party might be trying to provide an acceptable basis for Taruc's surrender and pardon. As the most popular Huk leader and Communist, he would be invaluable if he could move freely among the people. Until absolutely reliable evidence or proof to the contrary turned up, this possibility could not be disregarded.

Said an army intelligence officer shortly after Taruc was brought into headquarters, "He still talks like a Communist." After several days of conversation with Taruc following his surrender, José Crisol, the Under-Secretary of National Defense, said, "We have been brain-washing each other. So far I am not sure who is winning." This comment, partly in jest, nevertheless indicates that the government was taking the Taruc surrender with the caution that it deserved.

It is important to note that Taruc's capitulation followed the capture and surrender of many of his lieutenants in the Central Luzon Huk organization. One of these was Commander Laban, who had joined the first Huk units at the end of 1941 to fight the Japanese invaders. In recent years he has been the Huk mayor of the Candaba Swamp, an area some seven by fifteen miles in extent, which is under water during the rainy season but dries out in the summer. On the islands and in the tall grasses of this swamp the Huks often made their hideout. Commander Laban served as a contact man between the Huk fighting forces and the civilians in the barrios surrounding the swamp. His job was to assemble supplies and see that the Huk army was well fed. In the early years the civilians co-operated willingly and brought goods to the assembly points, but more recently they have been reluctant and unco-operative. Laban and his men have had to go from place to place and gather supplies, sometimes through a show of force.

One day early in May a brother of Commander Laban called at the army outpost on the eastern edge of the Candaba Swamp. The soldiers were quartered temporarily in the very schoolhouse which Taruc had attended as an elementary student. In a conversation with Captain Tecson, the brother explained that Laban was planning to attend the town fiesta in near-by San Miguel. The captain set up a check point on the road to the town and maintained a twenty-four-hour vigilance on all traffic. Three days later at midnight the guard stopped a cart and began to check the passengers. One of those on the front seat whispered that the man asleep on the floor of the cart was Commander Laban. The guard called Captain Tecson. The captain shook the man awake and asked him, "Are you Commander Laban?"

He replied, "No, you have the wrong party."

But his wife spoke up, "Yes, he is Commander Laban, and he is my husband."

Captain Tecson said, "All right, hand over your gun; your days with the Huks are now ended."

Laban replied, "I have no gun."

But his wife again interrupted, "Yes he does and here it is." She pulled a pistol from underneath a bale of hay and handed it to the captain.

Had Commander Laban been captured, or had he surrendered? The army intelligence men in reviewing the circumstances of the case were not sure. It could be that he wanted to surrender, but for fear of Huk reprisals wished to make it appear that he had been captured. At any rate, Commander Laban seemed willing to co-operate with the army in making contact with other Huk leaders. After several days of questioning by the intelligence officers, Captain Tecson asked that Laban be allowed to remain with the field unit where he could be used as a ready source of information. While in this position, Laban reported that for several months the Huk commanders in the lower levels and the men in the ranks had urged Taruc to work out some kind of peace with the government. He said that they were tired of fighting and running and being pursued; they wanted to live again in peace. Laban's statements agree with those of other Huks captured or surrendered in recent months. The existence of this desire to make terms with the government may have been a powerful factor in Taruc's decision to give up. Not only did he find himself cornered by the army forces but also he realized that his own men had lost the desire to continue fighting. The fact that he was losing his popular following must have been as potent an argument with Taruc as the military pressure of the government's armed forces.

The Huk movement is coming apart at the seams. The split is appearing precisely along the line where the popular peasant movement was sewn together with the Communist party. There is some evidence of a split within the inner circle of party leaders: between the Taruc brothers, who have been closest to the peasants, and the other Politburo members, who have been more rigid in adherence to the party line. Their mass support not only has deserted but in many instances has gone over to the government side and helped to round up the Huk fighters.

The success of the government's actions against the Huks can be dated from the capture of the Politburo on October 18, 1950. In reviewing the experience of the last four years, several important aspects of the successful campaign stand out: first, a vigorous and effective military action; second, the winning of the people to the government's side; third, an exposé of Communist ideas and the propagation of democratic principles; and fourth, attrition against the hard core of communism.

An essential prerequisite to the success of the campaign has been a group of capable national leaders devoted to the democratic way of life. These leaders have learned that military force alone could not suppress the Huk movement. A campaign of verbal propaganda for democracy by itself was not enough. Land reform alone, even according to Communist Politburo members, would not stop the armed rebellion. Success against the Huks could result only from a simultaneous attack on many fronts.

Military action became effective especially when it was combined with measures to improve public support. As long as the army was party to occasional acts of violence against the people in Huklandia, the civilians remained taciturn and hostile. However, a friendly army which gave the civilians protection against Huk raids and foraging parties won the respect of the people. The government learned that if its army provided peace and order both day and night it could retain the loyalty of the residents. The communication of pro-government sympathies in the war of ideas was most effective in the areas where the army had provided security for the people. Thus, the propaganda struggle went hand in hand with the military action.

Hard-hitting army units kept the Huks on the run. The constant pressure made their life as guerrillas difficult and discouraging. Without this military action undoubtedly the number of surrendered Huks would have been far less. Though the military force was negative, it was an effective measure when coupled with positive programs of attraction. The positive programs alone, such as EDCOR, would never have been sufficient to break up the Huk movement, but they could take the ex-Huks who had been separated from the movement and restore them to useful citizenship.

As the Huks became fewer, more disorganized, and discouraged, they held their fire and passed up opportunities to ambush army patrols. Sensitive army men were quick to note this situation. By May of 1954 the patrols were firing at theHuks only as a last resort. There were instances in the Central Luzon area where soldiers had chased down the fleeing Huks in open fields. The avoidance of useless bloodshed increased the popularity of the army throughout the area. It must be remembered that every Huk had numerous relatives among the civilian population. No matter what the cause, the killing of one's countrymen was not popular.

For too many years the government had been set apart from the common people in the farm lands of Central Luzon. Before the war, government positions were held by representatives of the landlord class, and their offices were conducted largely in behalf of that group. The peasants lived to themselves and nursed their grievances in secret meetings of their own organizations. During the Japanese occupation the Philippine government offered them no protection. At the end of the war the peasants felt no obligation to support the government nor to be loyal to it in the struggle with the Huks.

In this situation it took something more than a barrage of verbal propaganda to win the people. They wanted more than promises; they wanted tangible evidence that the government was on the side of justice and would act in the interest of the people's welfare. The improved record of the government in recent years has greatly strengthened the campaign against the Huks. For example, the Rice Share Tenancy Act, which for years had not been put into effect, recently has become the basis of settling tenant complaints through the Industrial Relations Courts. As the tenants become aware of the existence of this legal process of settling issues, increasing numbers of cases are brought to court. A new appreciation of law has developed among the common people. This is basic to a sound democracy. The EDCOR resettlement program, though far from a complete solution to the problems of landless farmers and peasant poverty, has been an important demonstration of the government's desire to help the people. In the face of these sincere efforts, individuals who had been sympathetic with the Huks or on the verge of casting their lot with the revolutionaries began to reconsider. Perhaps after all a government with a genuine humanitarian concern for the people was worth supporting.

The clean elections of 1951 and 1953 were major factors in winning the people to the side of democratic government. The chicanery during the 1949 election had created enough disaffection for the Communist party to declare that a revolutionary situation existed and that it was moving toward a revolutionary crisis, making possible the overthrow of the government by November 7, 1951. The party plans and the target date for the revolution were revealed in Politburo documents captured in 1950.[1]

The new Magsaysay administration, which was elected by an unprecedented majority in 1953, has started a vigorous program of national development. Beginning with the barrios where the majority of the people live, the program includes new roads, more sanitary wells, additional schools, antimalarial drives in the areas where this is a problem, financial aid to small farmers through agricultural credit co-operatives, and assistance in improved farming through agricultural extension services. In addition to the EDCOR farms, a greatly increased program of land settlement for thousands of land-hungry citizens is under way. The careful study and improvement of the services of many government bureaus will bring increased efficiency and confidence. The Philippine Congress has just approved a billion-peso bond issue to finance basic industrial development. This is part of a long-range program to give the nation a more balanced economy and to solve the problem of unemployment. The people take pride in the government which they put into office, and they have responded enthusiastically to the launching of these measures.

While engrossed in the conduct of government affairs, the Philippines has not overlooked the ideological challenge presented by communism. Communism spreads not only among workers and peasants who bear the brunt of social and economic maladjustments; it also spreads among the leaders of society: the lawyers, teachers, doctors, and intellectuals to whom ideas are important.

Democracy has an intellectual and moral advantage which it can ill afford to lose. The plausible intricacies of Marxist dialectics are more than matched with the realistic and demonstrable truths of democratic life. The people of any nation will respond to the challenge of an ideal, a cause, a mission. Every generation must be taught that democracy not only means a good life on a high level of living but primarily is a life of freedom in a land of opportunity, where merit is rewarded, where man is not penalized for believing in God, and where all the important decisions are not dictated by a handful of men in control of a political party. This is the challenge of democracy. This is what the Filipino people are fighting for; this is what the United Nations fought for in Korea. Sometimes the fight must be carried on with guns and bullets, but much of the struggle must be fought with words and ideas that contrast the stark oppression of Communist control in all its inhumanity with the picture of free democratic life in all its glorious possibilities.

The experience of the Philippines shows that steady progress against the Huks depended upon a thorough understanding of communism. The campaign could never be waged simply as a military field operation; it was always at the same time a battle of ideas. Government leaders had to know what communism is and how it works. The Huks could not be treated as local national dissidents; they had connections with the Communists elsewhere and reacted locally according to the international party line. Negotiations for truce, amnesty, or surrender ran into the same kind of stalling and double talk that became so infuriating at Panmunjom. In the Philippines the government leaders finally learned that negotiations for surrender are always used by the Huks for their own ulterior purposes. A genuine surrender is an impossibility, for surrender is interpreted by the Communists as admitting that the party is illegal. An individual Communist may leave the party or be expelled, but as long as he is a party member he must remain a revolutionary. The ultimate objective is the overthrow of the government, in which the party assumes that armed force is necessary. William Pomeroy, the American Communist who joined the Huks, explained that he did so because he wished to work in a situation where the revolution was more advanced than it was at home.

Communism can never be judged solely on the basis of what its leaders are saying and doing at the moment; it can only be judged in terms of its ultimate objectives. At any given point of time the party line might be "peace and co-operation." Such tactics are for purposes of preserving the movement and advancing to the next stage. Or, they may be designed to confuse the opposition. To pin a Communist down to a definite program is as difficult as striking the head of a twisting serpent.

Through years of experience in fighting the Communist aggression the administration leaders have reached a mature understanding of the nature of the opposing movement. Keenly aware of the slippery nature of Communist tactics, Major General Jesus Vargas, Chief of Staff of the Armed Forces of the Philippines, warned a Manila audience in a recent address: "We would be far from wise if we thought, as many would like to think today, that our Communist problem here had ended with the surrender of Taruc or will end with the capture, death, or surrender of the other Communist leaders. Communists are Communists. They have a way of shifting with ease from surface activities to underground movement, depending on the exigencies of the situation they are in. There is such a thing as a bloodless revolution, and that exactly is what the communists always pull on innocent democracies whenever they are not in a position to overthrow an enemy government militarily. With the return of the Communist leaders to peace, that kind of revo-

lution is what they will seek to wage. They will seek to associate
with worthy causes. They will adopt misleading party names
and alliances. They will maintain the 'hard core' of membership. They will enhance hatred and promote strikes and violence. They will resort to sabotage. They will seek to divide us.
Above all, they will infiltrate into the government, universi-
ties, civic organizations, even churches. That is the usual Communist pattern. With the Communist leaders back with us and
the masses, that is the problem we are up against." Without
such understanding of communism the victory which has been
gained in the armed struggle might be largely lost through the
infiltration tactics of "surrenderees" whose real party assignment was the "legal struggle." The government was handling
Taruc's case with great care to avoid this possible danger.

The hard-core Communists who are deeply indoctrinated
with the Marxist-Leninist-Stalinist-Mao theory are least amen-
able to prodemocratic ideas in the form of persuasion or literature. They may, however, be isolated from their following.
The government has had its greatest success in winning the mass
base away from the Huks and in the rehabilitation of the common Huk soldiers and Huk commanders, who largely compose
the settlers in the EDCOR farms. The loss of their mass support
places the inner core of Communist leaders under great pressure. They begin to question party policies and to quarrel
among themselves. In the face of failure some break away and
renounce communism, and others may be expelled as a matter
of party discipline. This has happened in the Communist party
of the Philippines in the past; present rumblings indicate that
it may happen again. After the armed revolt is completely
wiped out, the few hard-cored Communists who have been cut
off from their mass support can safely be left to die on the vine.

This indirect approach to communism, by winning the people away from their Communist leaders and leaving the hard
core isolated and hard pressed, has been the genius of the
Philippine program. A democratic appeal to the people can be
effective. Moreover, the appeal carries greatest force when it
is rooted in the experience of the people with representative
government in democratic communities and is not limited to
lectures and leaflets. EDCOR was effective in the anti-Huk
campaign not just because it was an idea that undercut the Huk

promises of "land for the landless" but primarily because it was an actual program of land settlement where democratic communities flourished. An experience in democracy is the real weapon against communism.

The lessons which the Philippines has learned in its struggle against communism have not come easily. They have been bathed in the blood and anguish of eight long years of civil strife since the end of World War II. But out of these struggles the government has developed an understanding of communism and has fashioned an effective program to strengthen its own democratic institutions. The Philippines has brought to the free world a victory and, more important, a way toward victory which may serve to aid and encourage other democracies that are locked in struggle with a Communist rebellion.

APPENDIX

NATIONAL ORGANIZATION OF THE COMMUNIST PARTY OF THE PHILIPPINES

CHART I
THE NATIONAL ADMINISTRATIVE COMMITTEES

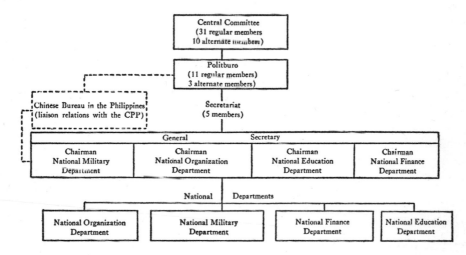

Source: Document captured by Task Force "GG" at Lagrimas, Twin Falls, Mount Dorst, August 12, 1951, based on "Political Resolution 12," March 1951 Central Committee Conference.

CHART II
MILITARY ORGANIZATION

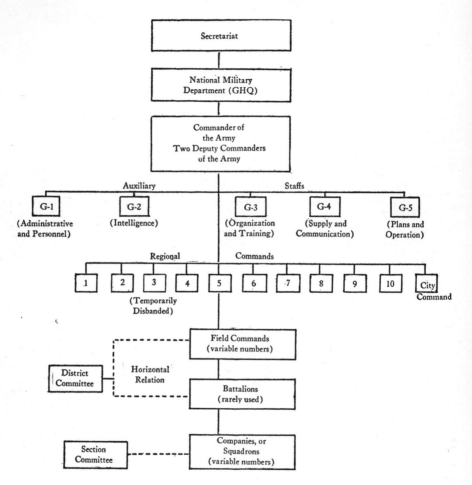

Source: "Military Resolution" issued by the Central Committee of May 15, 1951; document captured at Barrio Abo-Abo, Mauban, Quezon Province, by the 8th Battalion Combat Team on July 25, 1951.

CHART III
THE ORGANIZATION DEPARTMENT

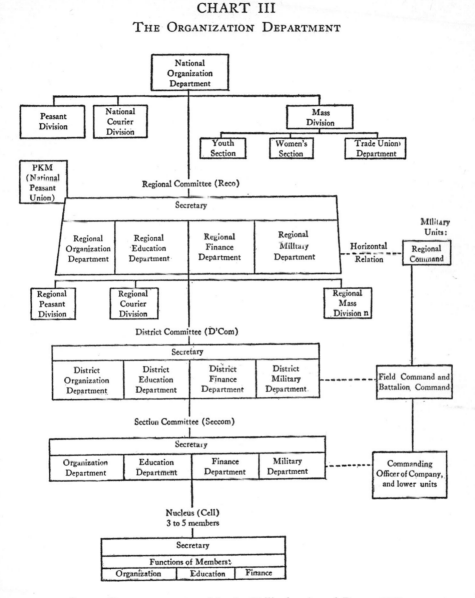

Source: Documents captured by the Philippine Armed Forces, 1951.

CHART IV
THE EDUCATION DEPARTMENT

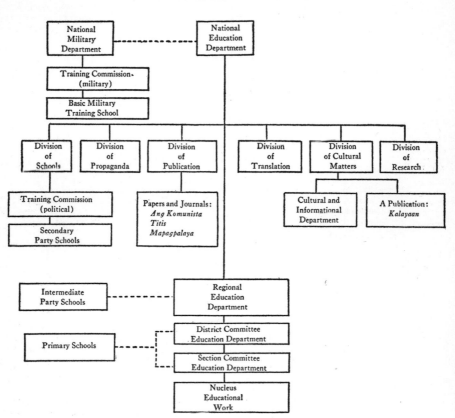

Source: "Organization Resolution 9," March 1951 Central Committee Conference.

CHART V
THE FINANCE DEPARTMENT

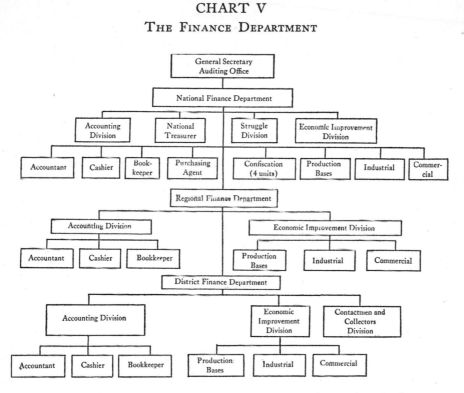

Source: "Political Resolution 10," of the March 1951 Central Committee Conference.

CHART VI

Party Control of Finances Through Interconnections Between Finance Committees and Political Committees at Various Levels of Party Organization

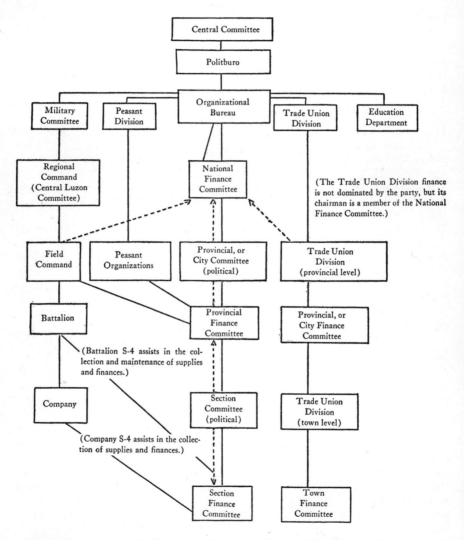

Source: Document originally produced by the chairman of the Finance Committee and captured by the Philippine Armed Forces, 1951.

NOTES

CHAPTER ONE

[1] Luis Taruc, *Born of the People* (New York: International Publishers, 1953), p. 63.

[2] *Ibid.*, pp. 129–30.

[3] Emiliano Morabe, "History of the Philippine Labor Movement," in *Department of Labor Yearbook* (Manila: Department of Labor, 1949), Vol. I, No. 1, pp. 32–38. In addition, uprisings are listed for the years 1629, 1660, 1744, 1823, and 1844.

[4] Emma H. Blair and James Alexander Robertson, *The Philippine Islands, 1493–1898* (Cleveland: Arthur H. Clark Company, 1909), Vol. 48, pp. 142–43.

[5] A revolt in 1660 in Pampanga is reported to have spread north into Pangasinan Province, Central Luzon, and to have involved some 40,000 men. *Ibid.*, Vol. 41, p. 58.

The revolt against Spain in 1896 was not only a nationalistic movement which kindled the sympathies of almost all Filipinos but also an agrarian uprising. The Katipunan led by Andres Bonafacio aimed to overthrow the Spanish government, but in fact his followers among the peasants of Luzon seized the lands controlled by the Spanish Friars. Many of the Friars were killed or driven away (Charles E. Derbyshire, translator's introduction to José Rizal, *The Social Cancer* [Manila: Philippine Education Company, 1912], first English edition, pp. xxxviii ff.). When the American forces came to the Philippines in 1898, this revolt was well under way. The force of the rebellion was redirected toward the Americans, whose control replaced the hated Spanish rule in the eyes of many Filipinos.

In the early 1920's occurred the Colorum movement, which was anticlerical but which had overtones of agrarian unrest (Joseph R. Hayden, *The Philippines, A Study in National Development* [New York: The Macmillan Company, 1942], p. 379). A more serious uprising occurred in the early 1930's under the auspices of a peasant party named Tangulan. This organization, secretly formed and directed by a Manila attorney, at one time numbered some 97,000 followers. In December 1931 they seized control of a town in Northern Luzon, but were able to hold it for only twenty-four hours. Several hundred of their leaders were apprehended and jailed in Manila, and the organization collapsed (*ibid.*, p. 915). See also Patricio Dionisio, "Labor Organizations in the Philippines, 1902–1935," a typescript copy of an unpublished report by a special investigator for the Department of Labor, The Philippines, 1936, pp. 16–20. The investigator, Dionisio, was the same attorney who had organized the Tangulan.

The Sakdals, a term meaning "to strike," were organized by Benigno Ramos, an anti-Quezon politician. The Sakdals included many of the same people who had been active in the Tangulan. Their ideas were partly nationalistic; they stood for immediate independence. Later they became pro-Japanese. They made a strong appeal to the peasants on the grounds that they were exploited by landlords and the politicians, whose grip could not be broken until the Philippines had achieved complete independence. In the 1934 elections the Sakdals staged an armed revolt in a futile effort to prevent the initiation of the Commonwealth Government (Joseph R. Hayden, *op. cit.,* pp. 382–400). After this show of force the government suppressed the movement. Its remnants co-operated with the Japanese invaders in 1942. Ramos was killed during the liberation struggle in 1945.

[6] "Report of the Fact Finding Survey of Rural Problems by the Department of Labor to the President of the Philippines," January 21, 1937 (unpublished). To this report, which covered conditions during 1936, was added the "Report of the Agrarian Commission to the President of the Philippines" (unpublished), showing that conditions as of June 1946 were about the same as they had been a decade earlier. These observations agree with those of Karl J. Pelzer, *Pioneer Land Settlement in the Asiatic Tropics* (New York: American Geographic Society, 1948), "Land Tenure Conditions at the Outbreak of War in the Pacific," pp. 91–104.

[7] Generoso F. Rivera and Robert T. McMillan, *The Rural Philippines,* (Manila: Office of Information, Mutual Security Agency, 1952), p. 157:

"The main characteristics of local government can be summarized as follows:

"1. Political leadership usually is centered in, or controlled by, small groups of large landowners, many of whom live in the poblaciones [the central cities of administrative areas], or other cities.

"2. With the dominant position of the family in the Filipinos' scheme of values, the government often becomes an object of exploitation in its behalf through nepotism, estafa [swindling], non-payment of taxes, and so forth.

"3. Differences of personal qualities rather than of economic interests or issues tend to be the basis for choosing political leaders.

"4. Custom and personal discretion frequently supersede statute law in the administration of government, especially when a law, such as the Rice Share Tenancy Act or Minimum Wage Law, adversely affects the economic interests of the landed group.

"5. Government officials generally are related by kinship or ideological ties to landed families.

"6. The average citizen of the barrio has little faith in the government, possibly because his participation in it and benefits from it are nominal.

"7. The taxation system strongly favors the land-owning class.

"A unique characteristic of the barrio is its almost complete lack of legal self-government. A municipality is a legal entity consisting ordinarily of a poblacion and from 15 to 30 or more barrios. As a part of the municipality, citizens of a barrio participate in the election of a mayor and council who, in turn, can enact ordinances which must be approved by the Provincial Board.

"As a political unit, the barrio is without legislative, executive, or judicial powers. The barrio lieutenant, a nominal counterpart of the pre-Spanish Cabeza de Barangay, is appointed by the municipal mayor although in practice the appointee usually is chosen first informally by residents of the barrio. This person serves without compensation and has no prescribed official duties. His principal functions are to assist the mayor in enforcing ordinances, settling petty disputes, raising funds for the annual fiesta, Red Cross, and other drives, and entertaining visitors."

[8] Patricio Dionisio, *op. cit.,* pp. 13–14. The 1924 date is preferred over the

1925 date given by Dionisio on the basis of the account in Dapen Liang, *The Development of Philippine Political Parties* (Hong Kong: South China Morning Post, 1939), p. 256, which is corroborated also by the typescript copy of "Interview with Cirilo Bognot," p. 1. Bognot was a labor leader and early member of the Communist group in the Philippines. He represented the local organization in Communist international gatherings and spent some time in Moscow in 1928 in training. During the 1930's he left the party. He died in Manila in 1954.

[9] Dapen Liang, *op. cit.,* p. 256.

[10] José Lava, *Milestones in the History of the Communist Party of the Philippines* (typescript copy of the mimeographed material used by the Communist party in its Huk training schools, a document captured by the Philippine Army), pp. 8–9. Since the action of the Congreso Obrero following this conference did not take place until 1927, the author feels some uncertainty about the accuracy of the 1925 invitation date.

[11] *Ibid.,* p. 8; see also the Philippine Army pamphlet, *Our Enemy* (based on captured Huk documents and mimeographed for intelligence briefing purposes), p. 2. Both sources agree that Tan Malacca was the agent for the invitation.

[12] From a stenographic report of the questioning of Tan Malacca at the Bureau of Customs, following his arrest and during the deportation proceedings. *Manila Daily Bulletin,* August 16, 1927.

[13] According to Cirilo Bognot (*op. cit.,* p. 3), Malacca had studied in Moscow in 1920 but had "taken a firm stand against the majority opinion at the Fourth Comintern Congress at Leningrad in November, 1922."

[14] *Manila Daily Bulletin*, August 16, 1927.

[15] *Ibid.,* August 15–20, 1927, carry stories of Tan Malacca.

[16] Cirilo Bognot (*op. cit.,* p. 2). The date for the beginning of the Workers' party has been revised to conform with the account in José Lava (*op. cit.,* p. 11), which seems to fit into the other related dates of this period of the development of the radical movement.

[17] José Lava, *op. cit.,* p. 11.

[18] Author's interview with Federico Maclang, convicted Politburo member serving sentence at New Bilibid Prison, Muntinglupa, March 17, 1954. Manahan was killed by the Japanese in 1942.

[19] Patricio Dionisio, *op. cit.,* p. 10.

[20] José Lava, *op. cit.,* p. 12; also Fortunato L. Crisologo, *The Present Educational Practices of the Huks* (unpublished Master's thesis, University of the Philippines, 1953), pp. 1–2.

[21] Crisologo, *op. cit.,* pp. 2–3. The organizing committee was composed of Crisanto Evangelista, Antonio D. Ora, Arturo Soriano, Jacinto Manahan, and José Quirante.

[22] "Reports of Cases Determined in the Supreme Court of the Philippine Islands," *Philippine Reports* (Manila: Bureau of Printing, 1935), Vol. 57, p. 256.

[23] *Ibid.,* p. 257.

[24] *Ibid.,* p. 373.

[25] Crisanto Evangelista, *Communism and Capitalism* (Manila, 1932). This book, printed in English and Tagalog, summarizes the charges made against the Communists and the defense which Crisanto Evangelista himself presented

in behalf of the twenty-seven men. His was a strange defense in that he admitted frankly to most of the charges but then presented a lengthy brief explaining the kind of revolution and class war the Communist party stood for, and justifying it by reference to the course of history and a Marxist prediction of the decay and downfall of capitalism. Evangelista's statement reads more like a propaganda piece than the legal defense it was supposed to be.

[26] Author's interviews with Quirino Abad Santos and with various individuals who had known Pedro Abad Santos during the 1930's. One of these was the wife of Agapito del Rosario, who nursed Pedro Abad Santos during the last few months of his life.

[27] Dapen Liang, *op. cit.*, p. 255, based on the *Manila Times Weekly*, June 4, 1916.

[28] Quirino Abad Santos, "The Historical Background of the Huk Movement," *The Philippine Journal of Education*, Vol. XXXII, No. 9, March 1954.

[29] José Lava, *Twenty Years of Struggle of the Communist Party of the Philippines* (typescript copy of the mimeographed material used in the Huk training schools and captured by the Philippine Army), p. 3. Lava, who writes under the alias "Gregorio Santayana," states that following the imprisonment of the Communist leaders, "The exploited peasants and workers did not take such action lying down. The Communist Party of the Philippines went underground and directed the legal struggle of the masses of peasants and workers from underground. At the same time, Comrade Pedro Abad Santos organized the Socialist Party of the Philippines in 1932 to carry on the legal struggle of the exploited masses which the Communist Party of the Philippines can not do very effectively because of its outlawing. Even from the very inception, the Socialist Party of the Philippines was never intended to be like the Blum or Thomas socialist parties. The name 'Socialist' was adopted as a mere tactical maneuver to permit legal existence at a time when the Communist Party of the Philippines was outlawed. . . . With the release of the communist leaders [in 1938], negotiations were immediately begun for the merger of the Communist and Socialist Parties which really had no fundamental differences. With the help of Comrade Allen of the American Communist Party, the merger was finally ratified in the Party Convention held in 1938."

[30] José Lava, *Milestones in the History of the Communist Party of the Philippines*, p. 10:

"With the organization of the Socialist Party of the Philippines and the AMT [Peasant Union] there immediately arose ideological as well as organizational differences concerning forms of organization and methods of struggle between the CPP and the SPP. One of the most important differences arose regarding the correct organizational structure of the AMT. The AMT was composed of peasants and agricultural and industrial workers. The CPP took the position that the workers, as the rising class in our developing capitalist economy, should be organized separately from the peasants, considering that they are really different classes. On the other hand, the SPP claimed that the peasants of Central Luzon were very poor, property-less and extremely exploited, no less than workers of existing industries, and that they were far more militant than any other group of toilers. In organizing the poor peasants and workers into a single national workers union, the socialists claimed that the workers were organized separately in their own organizations and merely affiliated with the AMT. It is obvious that in the difference of opinion between the socialists and the Communists both committed errors of theory and organization. The socialists failed to grasp clearly the leading role of the proletariat, considering the poor peasants as equally revolutionary as, if not more so than, the workers. On the other hand, the Communists committed the error of thinking that because of the different class character of peasants and workers, peasants' and workers' organizations should not be affiliated with a common mother organization like the AMT. It was only necessary to recognize and project the leading role of the proletariat in such organizational alliance.

"Another serious disagreement was the lack of differentiation between the party and the mass organization as far as the SPP and the AMT were concerned. Following the well-known Leninist concept of the Communist Party as the vanguard of the working class, the communists made a clear distinction between the CPP on the one hand and mass organizations on the other; but the socialists did not make any distinction between the SPP and the AMT. Because of the failure to make such distinction, AMT mass members were considered as members also of the SPP. This explains the lack of organizational life and loose organizational procedures and discipline within the SPP. Such looseness and anarchy in organization were brought by the socialists into the merged Communist and Socialist Parties [1938].

"Still another serious conflict was in the method of conducting mass struggles and mass actions. The Communists had a tendency to be too legalistic, especially after the outlawing of the CPP. Instead of leading the masses in militant and direct mass actions to give them valuable revolutionary experiences, as the socialists did, they had a tendency to project the legalistic methods of struggle. On the other hand, the socialists, notwithstanding some errors of 'leftism' and sectarianism, led the exploited peasants and workers in militant and direct struggle and mass actions, giving their masses better revolutionary experiences devoid of legalistic illusions."

[31] "Tenants' Legislation Adopted by the Socialist Party of the Philippines," an undated document in the author's possession, the actual date probably being 1935, a year of great Socialist party activity, and a time of agrarian unrest that provoked President Quezon to formulate his "social justice" program.

[32] José Lava, *op. cit.,* p. 14.

[33] Luis Taruc, *op. cit.,* p. 42.

[34] Quoted in Eusebio Macaspac Manuel, *Manual for the Study of the Hukbalahap Problem* (unpublished Master's thesis, Silliman University, 1948), p. 69.

[35] *Ibid.,* p. 36. The author, Manuel, was, at the time he made the observation, a mature man and a Protestant minister in Central Luzon.

[36] *Ibid.,* pp. 63–66.

[37] *Ibid.,* pp. 72–73.

[38] *Ibid.,* p. 154.

[39] Certified copy of "absolute pardon" for Crisanto Evangelista, National Bureau of Prisons, Muntinglupa, Philippines.

[40] José Lava, *op. cit.,* p. 11.

[41] "Opinions of the Secretary of Justice," Opinion No. 19, Series 1939, quoted in Special Committee on Un-Filipino Activities, House of Representatives, *Report on the Illegality of the Communist Party of the Philippines* (Manila: Bureau of Printing, 1951), pp. 62 ff. At the request of the Secretary

of Labor, the Secretary of Justice wrote an opinion which legalized the Katipunan ng mga Anak Pawis sa Filipinas (Society of the Children of Sweat). This is the Communist labor union which had been declared illegal by the Manila Court of First Instance in the 1931 Communist trials. In the review of the decision the following year by the Supreme Court the decision of the lower court was affirmed in general but only the Communist party of the Philippines was specifically declared illegal by the Supreme Court. Regardless of the legal interpretations involved in these cases the fact remained that in 1939 the labor organizations which the Communists had organized a decade earlier were again able to operate legally. Through similar legal interpretations the Popular Front party, including the Communist party of the Philippines, had by 1941 achieved legal standing with all the rights provided by law for minority parties.

[42] José Lava, *op. cit.,* p. 11.

[43] "Constitution of the Communist Party of the Philippines," reproduced in *Our Enemy,* pp. 6–15; also José Lava, *op. cit.,* p. 11.

[44] *Report on the Illegality of the Communist Party of the Philippines,* p. 75, quoting from J. Ozaeta, "Dissenting Opinion in the Case of Juan Sumulong in his Capacity as President of the Popular Front (Sumulong), Petitioner, versus The Commission on Elections, Respondent, G.R. No. 48634, Promulgated October 8, 1941," in which the Supreme Court affirmed a decision of the Commission on Elections granting the Popular Front party, headed by Pedro Abad Santos, the exclusive right to propose the minority election inspector in the second congressional district of Pampanga for the 1941 elections.

[45] Luis Taruc, *op. cit.,* p. 49; also Joseph R. Hayden, *op. cit.,* p. 451.

[46] José Lava, *Twenty Years of Struggle of the Communist Party of the Philippines,* p. 7.

[47] *Our Enemy,* p. 86, quoting a written statement by Luis Taruc.

[48] José Lava, *op. cit.,* p. 10.

[49] Author's interview with the wife of Vicente Lava. Mrs. Lava and her children remained in Manila during the war.

[50] Luis Taruc, *op. cit.,* p. 53.

[51] Eusebio Macaspac Manuel, *op. cit.,* p. 41. The author was the one who talked with Taruc.

[52] Luis Taruc, *op. cit.,* p. 209, quoting a statement by Mariano Balgos, entitled, "Where We Stand," and delivered in Manila on June 15, 1945. The international Communist movement has attempted to present the Huk revolt as a respectable revolution. The author has compared the original manuscript of Taruc's autobiography, which was partly written by William Pomeroy (according to Pomeroy and his wife), with the actual volume printed by International Publishers in New York. Besides the usual changes in phrasing and deletions for the sake of style, many entire sections of material describing in detail how collaborators and enemies of the Huks among the Filipino people were liquidated were omitted. If these descriptions were left in the story as they were originally written, the Huks would appear much more like ruthless Communists than harmless agrarian reformers. Apparently, the editors knew best what an English-reading public would prefer to hear. See also Maximo Giron, *Report on Communism in the Philippines* (Manila: The Manila Courier, 1946), pp. 292–93.

[53] Author's interview with one who must remain anonymous but who was an active leader in the Huk organization during the war.

CHAPTER TWO

[1] Highly critical accounts of American policy during the period of liberation are: Hernando J. Abaya, *Betrayal in the Philippines* (New York: A. A. Wyn, Inc., 1946) and Bernard Seeman and Laurence Salisbury, *Cross Currents in the Philippines* (New York: Institute of Pacific Relations, Pamphlet No. 23, 1946). Also critical but more reliable are Lawrence K. Rosinger, "The Philippines—Problems of Independence," *Foreign Policy Reports* (New York: Foreign Policy Association, September 1, 1948); Shirley Jenkins, "Great Expectations in the Philippines," *Far Eastern Survey* (New York: Institute of Pacific Relations, August 13, 1947); and David Bernstein, *The Philippine Story* (New York: Farrar, Strauss and Company, 1947), chapter on "The Politics of Liberation."

[2] Armed Forces of the Philippines, "Annual Report of the Chief of Staff, July 1, 1947–June 30, 1948" (unpublished), pp. 22–23.

[3] Armed Forces of the Philippines, "Annual Report of the Chief of Staff, 1946" (unpaged typescript).

[4] Armed Forces of the Philippines, *Today* (Christmas Issue, 1952), p. 36.

[5] Eusebio Macaspac Manuel, *Manual for the Study of the Hukbalahap Problem,* p. 36, describes the two antisocialist organizations started by Pablo Angeles David and other landlords during the 1930's. These were called Batung Maputi (White Stone) and Kawal sing Kapayapan (Soldiers of Peace).

[6] Philippine Army, Intelligence Report, October 14, 1946, Bamban, Tarlac.

[7] Based on correspondence from the private files of a Manila newspaperman.

[8] PKM stands for Pambansang Kaisahan ng mga Magbubukid (National Peasants' Union). This organization, founded in 1946, united two previous peasant groups: the KPMP, Katipunan Pambansa ng mga Magbubukid sa Filipinas (National Union of Peasants in the Philippines), a Communist union dating from the early 1920's, and the AMT, Aguman Ding Maldeng Talapegobra (Workers and Peasants' Union), a socialist union dating from the early 1930's. The PKM gave the Huks a united mass base among the peasants of Central Luzon.

[9] Public Relations Office, Philippine Constabulary, "Press Statement of the President on the Outlawing of the Hukbalahap and the PKM" (1948), p. 1.

[10] Events leading up to the amnesty and its aftermath may be found in the following issues of the *Manila Chronicle,* 1948: Jan. 11, Feb. 5, May 14, June 21–22, Aug. 31, Sept. 5, 7, 10–12, 16, 21. Members of this newspaper staff were participant-observers in these negotiations; thus the news releases are first-hand reports.

[11] José Lava, *Milestones in the History of the Communist Party of the Philippines,* pp. 28–29.

[12] In the period immediately following the war, the Communist party and its armed branch, the Huks, joined with liberal and progressive groups to form the Democratic Alliance. This was a political organization which opposed Manuel Roxas and supported President Sergio Osmeña in the first postwar elections. The Democratic Alliance ran candidates for legislative posts from the Central Luzon provinces. From this area six Democratic Alliance candidates were elected to the Congress in 1946. All of them, plus one Nacionalista congressman and three nacionalista senators, were refused seats by the legislature, which was under the control of the Liberal party (Roxas).

[13] Fortunato L. Crisologo, *The Present Educational Practices of the Huks,* pp. 25–26, based on captured Huk documents.

[14] William Pomeroy, "Pomeroy's Own Story" (unpublished account captured by the Philippine Army at the time of the capture of Pomeroy), p. 6.

[15] Philippine Army, *Our Enemy,* Chap. VI, "Biographies," pp. 70–130, based on "Self-Analysis," by Communist party members, documents among those captured from the Huks. Also, author's own interviews, 1954, of twenty-four Politburo members serving jail sentences at the National Prison, Muntinglupa.

[16] Armed Forces of the Philippines, *Order of Battle,* (based on captured enemy document, January 1952), p. 224.

[17] *Our Enemy,* p. 27.

[18] *Order of Battle* (document of August 1952), p. A 226a.

[19] "Such was the situation when the Party held its enlarged Politburo Conference in January, 1950. The conference confirmed the existence of a revolutionary situation; placed the entire Party under military discipline; adopted the RECO (Regional Command) organizational arrangements; and distributed its top leaders among the RECO's, to supervise the strengthening of the RECOs and the decisive implementation of military-organizational expansion plans of the Party. It declared that the next two years would be most crucial in the history of our country, and adopted the action slogan of 'all for expansion and the armed struggle' as a means to prepare for the seizure of power on a national scale. Finally, the conference decided to convert our guerrilla forces into a regular army, and launch coordinated military actions on a wide scale." José Lava, *Twenty Years of Struggle of the Communist Party of the Philippines,* pp. 21–22.

[20] Report of Major Conrado Uichanco, quoted in the *Philippine Free Press,* September 23, 1950.

[21] From information supplied by the Military History Section, Information and Education, General Headquarters, Armed Forces of the Philippines.

[22] An excellent account of these prewar efforts at resettlement is found in Karl J. Pelzer, *Pioneer Land Settlement in the Asiatic Tropics,* pp. 127–59.

[23] Republic Act No. 591, Section 3.

[24] The Economic Development Corps was established December 15, 1950, under the Chief of Staff, Armed Forces of the Philippines. The chief functions of EDCOR are:

"a. The taking over of surrendered or captured dissidents, who are neither indicted nor convicted by civil courts, for the purpose of resettlement and reeducating them in democratic, peaceful, and productive ways of life.

"b. The resettlement of selected ex-servicemen, ex-guerrillas, and ex-trainees, and other selected Filipino citizens, in EDCOR Farms as a means of utilizing them as stabilizing influence in the reeducation and reformation of ex-dissidents taken over by EDCOR as settlers.

"c. The training of surrendered or captured dissidents in the various trades and occupations for the purpose of enabling them to pursue gainful occupations." Armed Forces of the Philippines, *Troop Information,* Pamphlet No. 21, p. 3.

CHAPTER THREE

[1] *Manila Bulletin,* March 29, 1954 (Anniversary Edition), "Mindanao Still Land of Promise," Section III, pp. 2–5.

[2] Armed Forces of the Philippines, *Today,* October 1951, p. 14.

[3] Information supplied by Office of the Chief of EDCOR, Camp Crame, Philippines.

[4] Statement by Dr. James Meader, Chief Public Affairs Officer, United States Embassy, Manila.

[5] Figures supplied by Farm Administration, Arevalo EDCOR Farm, Kapatagan, Lanao.

[6] E. L. Cross, unpublished report on Buldon EDCOR Farm, June 18, 1952. Also, historical records supplied by Farm Administration, Gallego EDCOR Farm, Buldon, Cotabato.

[7] The list of physical properties at the first settlement at Kapatagan is equally impressive: "Today the Arevalo EDCOR Farm in Kapatagan is as good as, if not better than, any progressive community in the Philippines. It has, among other things, an administration building, a half dozen enlisted men's barracks which house soldiers providing protection, an enlisted men's mess hall, several hundred settlers' huts with latrines, a school house, a chapel, a hospital, a bachelor officers' quarters, a library, a cooperative store, a power house, a nursery building, a poultry administration building, numerous poultry sheds, piggery buildings, motor pool sheds, a guest house, adequate pitcher-type pumps, a guard house, and even an airfield. Moreover the settlement has a movie projector, a radio phone, a radio phonograph, a public address system reaching the settlers' huts, and two electric generators that furnish light to all the houses." Armed Forces of the Philippines, *Troop Information,* Pamphlet 21, p. 6.

[8] A good description and appraisal of the prewar efforts of the National Land Settlement Administration in the Koronadal Valley, Cotabato, Mindanao, under the leadership of Major General Paulino Santos is found in Karl J. Pelzer, *Pioneer Land Settlement in the Asiatic Tropics,* pp. 141–59.

[9] Armed Forces of the Philippines, "Mimeographed Procedure for Selection of Non-ex-HMB Settlers for Admission to EDCOR Farms, April 21, 1953."

[10] Armed Forces of the Philippines, "Settlers Contract."

[11] Armed Forces of the Philippines, *Troop Information,* Pamphlet 21, p. 4.

CHAPTER FOUR

[1] All the stories in this chapter are based on case studies of a random sample of 50 per cent of the ex-Huks and suspects at the EDCOR farms at Buldon and Kapatagan in Mindanao. Interviews were made by the author on the field during September and November, 1953. All names of settlers have been changed in order to prevent any possible embarrassment or danger to them.

[2] William Pomeroy and his wife, Celia Mariano Pomeroy, were both assigned to the Educational Bureau. Trained as a writer, Pomeroy produced manuals for use in the Huk schools and propaganda leaflets. He edited and polished Taruc's autobiography, *Born of the People,* published over Taruc's own signature in 1953 by International Publishers, New York.

[3] José Nava died of illness in 1954 while serving his sentence in prison. His trial had followed that of the Manila Politburo members during mid-1951.

[4] Although the public schools in the Philippines are "free" in the sense that they do not cost as much to attend as a private school, nevertheless, the cost of books, paper, pencils, medical fees, and fees for high-school enrollment do raise a barrier between education and the lowest-income families. When the Huks promised free schools, they appealed to those who wanted completely free edu-

cation, especially through the elementary grades. What the Huks delivered, however, was not education in the important sense of "free education," but indoctrination.

[5] Figures based on the author's own survey.

[6] See Note 8, Chapter II.

[7] In an effort to facilitate the army's efforts to break up the Huk resistance, President Quirino suspended the writ of habeas corpus, Proclamation No. 210, October 22, 1950. The writ was restored near the end of his term in office in December 1953.

CHAPTER FIVE

[1] The rat problem became so bad in Cotabato at the end of the rice season in 1953 that thousands of families left their farms and the province. Other thousands faced starvation. Newspapers and magazines were filled with articles discussing the problem in late 1953 and 1954. Congress appropriated funds to fight the rats. President Magsaysay declared an emergency in Cotabato Province and sent army teams to help in the campaign of eradication. Rat extermination experts were imported from abroad. The Philippine Red Cross, United Nations relief, and CARE packages helped to feed the people. Although the EDCOR farms were outside the areas of worst infestation, a few of the settlers lost most of their harvest to the rats.

[2] Recruiting officials and politicians in some instances made irresponsible promises of giving the settlers carabaos and plows, but the EDCOR administration promised only to furnish these and charge the cost to the settler's account.

CHAPTER SIX

[1] During March 1953 there were two conferences with the farm administrator over land claims, according to records in the historical section of Buldon EDCOR Farm.

Although the squatter problem is to be found in many parts of Mindanao, it is especially severe in Cotabato Province. Here the desire for new land has been great, and the possibility of gaining titles is slim. In the year ending July 1, 1951, in Cotabato Province only 509 titles were granted out of 3,403 applications. Before land is available for homesteading it must be released by the Bureau of Forestry. This agency has not reclassified any land since prewar days. A high provincial official (in a report not for publication) said that all the good land is owned by somebody with influence. "Many of these speculators are absentee landlords basking in their swivel chairs in Manila, Cebu, or Negros. The choicest lands along the highway have already been allocated to these speculators. When an immigrant comes seeking public land, he is sent thirty to fifty miles into the hinterland. The poor immigrant gets discouraged, packs up his things and leaves." Or he squats on a piece of land and hopes that somehow he can secure a title to it.

[2] The farming is according to the *kaingin* system, whereby the trees and brush are cut down and burned and the area planted for a year or two until the grass takes over. Then the *kaingin* is abandoned for another area in the forest, and the process is repeated.

[3] This is a joint appropriation made by the United States through the FOA (Foreign Operations Administration) and the PHILCUSA (Philippine Council for United States Aid). *Manila Times,* September 22, 1953.

CHAPTER SEVEN

[1] Generoso F. Rivera and Robert T. McMillan, *The Rural Philippines*, pp. 14, 102.

[2] See the well-known accounts by José Rizal, *The Social Cancer,* and *The Reign of Greed* (Manila: Philippine Education Company, 1912—first printing in English).

[3] Karl J. Pelzer, *Pioneer Settlement in the Asiatic Tropics,* pp. 88–89.

[4] Dean C. Worcester, *The Philippines Past and Present* (New York: The Macmillan Company, 1914), Vol. II, pp. 676–78. Worcester follows the report of Morga, *Sucesos de las Islas Filipinas* (Rizal's 1890 edition), reflecting conditions in the Philippines during the time of Morga's stay in the islands, 1595 to about 1608. Morga describes the various classes of slaves and has this to say about the relation of the problem to indebtedness: "Loans with interest were in very common practice, excessively high rates of interest being current, so that the debt doubled and multiplied all the time during which the payment was deferred, until there was taken from the debtor what he possessed as capital, and, when ultimately nothing more was left, his person and his children."

[5] Dean C. Worcester, *Slavery and Peonage in the Philippine Islands* (Manila: Bureau of Printing, 1913), 120 pp. This report of the Secretary of the Interior of the Philippines at that time stirred up a storm of protest that there was no such thing as slavery in the Philippines, but Worcester's documentary evidence in the form of sworn statements by Filipino officials and by Americans stationed in the provinces, offers convincing proof of the existence of the practice, especially the enslaving of individuals from the pagan tribes.

[6] Commonwealth Act No. 178, known as the Rice Share Tenancy Act, was approved November 13, 1936. It was made effective in the five Central Luzon provinces by proclamation of President Manuel Quezon on January 20, 1937. Karl Pelzer (*Pioneer Land Settlement in the Philippines,* p. 101), after tracing the practice under this act and its various amendments prior to World War II, shows that it "failed to regulate relations between landlord and tenant."

The Rice Share Tenancy Act was again amended in 1946 by Republic Act No. 34, in which tenants under certain conditions were favored with a 70-30 crop sharing arrangement. Robert S. Hardie, *Philippine Land Tenure Reform, Analysis and Recommendations* (Manila: Mutual Security Agency 1952), Appendix G 33.

On the basis of extensive field surveys in 1951–52, Rivera and McMillan reported, "The Philippine Rice Share Tenancy Act and other legislation that regulates landlord-tenant agreements probably have effected slight improvement of crop sharing practices from the standpoint of tenants, but the law generally is unenforced and its principles disregarded" (Generoso F. Rivera and Robert T. McMillan, *op. cit.,* p. 118). The new Nacionalista administration under President Ramon Magsaysay in 1954 immediately undertook to strengthen the administration of the Rice Share Tenancy Act by encouraging tenants to bring cases of violation to the courts.

[7] Emma Helen Blair and James Alexander Robertson (editors), *The Philippine Islands, 1493–1898,* Vol. 16, pp. 155–56. The note quoted from *Recopilación de Leyes* (Felipe II, Madrid, June 11, 1594), indicates that the assimilation of pre-Spanish social organization attained legal sanction by the Spanish authorities: "It is not right that the Indian chiefs of Filipinas be in a worse condition after conversion; rather should they have such treatment that would gain their affection and keep them loyal, so that with the spiritual bless-

ings that God has communicated to them by calling them to His true knowledge, the temporal blessings may be joined, and they may live contentedly and comfortably. Therefore, we order the governors of those islands to show them good treatment and entrust them, in our name, with the government of the Indians, of whom they were formerly the lords. In all else the governors shall see that the chiefs are benefited justly, and the Indians shall pay them something as a recognition, as they did during the period of their paganism, provided it be without prejudice to the tributes that are to be paid us, or prejudice to that which pertains to their encomenderos."

[8] Dean C. Worcester, *The Philippines Past and Present,* Vol. II, pp. 836–38; and Karl J. Pelzer, *op. cit.,* p. 91. The Congress of the United States granted authority to the Philippine Commission in 1902 to pass the Friar Lands Act, under which purchase was to be made of the Friar estates and the land redistributed to the tenants. Purchase of some of the estates was finally negotiated in 1905, but the Friars refused to sell all their holdings.

For legislation regarding agrarian problems, see Note 6, above, relating to the "social justice" program.

Joseph Rallston Hayden, *The Philippines,* p. 721. The Philippine Government (in Commonwealth Act No. 441, June 3, 1935) created a corporation known as the National Land Settlement Administration, with ₱20,000,000 appropriated for its capital stock. This corporation planned settlements on the homestead principle in the Compostela-Monkayo region north of Davao City in Mindanao, in the Kidapauan Valley northwest of Davao, and in the Koronadal Valley to the west and south of Davao. The purpose of these settlements was twofold: to develop the rich agricultural area of Southern Mindanao, and to encircle the Japanese colony at Davao and prevent its continued growth. The first of these colonies had been started in the Koronadal Valley before World War II.

[9] General Headquarters, Armed Forces of the Philippines, Camp Murphy, "Memorandum for All EDCOR Farm Administrators," August 11, 1952.

CHAPTER EIGHT

[1] Generoso F. Rivera and Robert T. McMillan, *The Rural Philippines,* p. 216.

[2] Figures from the office of the Kapatagan EDCOR Farm.

[3] From the articles by settlers in the "Souvenir Program," First Anniversary, Buldon EDCOR Farm, Cotabato, February 13–14, 1953.

[4] Data on the area around the Kapatagan EDCOR Farm contained in a report by the farm administrator to headquarters, Camp Crame, December 21, 1953.

[5] Figures furnished by the clinic, Buldon EDCOR farm.

[6] Figures furnished by the school principals, Buldon and Kapatagan elementary schools.

CHAPTER NINE

[1] Court of First Instance, Manila, "The Politburo Decision," 1951, p. 2.

[2] *Ibid.,* p. 41.

[3] José Lava, "Memorandum on the Causes of and Solution to Dissidence in the Philippines" (May 1, 1951, unpublished), p. 28.

[4] *Ibid.,* p. 41.

[5] *EDCOR,* a mimeographed Huk pamphlet in Tagalog.

[6] Captured Huks reported that in an effort to counter the latest government drive to eliminate the Huk forces, Casto Alejandrino, Huk army commander, "has ordered that all Huks who pick up, read, or use any of the surrender leaflets dropped by the armed forces be shot on sight." *Manila Times,* March 9, 1954.

CHAPTER TEN

[1] Among the top Huk leaders now serving life prison sentences at the national prison at Muntinglupa, José Lava and William Pomeroy are notable examples of the minority who became Communists almost solely on the basis of an intellectual experience.

[2] The testimony to this effect in Taruc's biography (*Born of the People,* p. 129) was amply corroborated in the interviews of ex-Huks at EDCOR.

[3] A schedule of questions was used in the interviewing. Each question was asked as it was written. When the individual did not understand English, a written translation of the questions in his dialect was used instead. Often the original question obtained only a partial response. In these instances the question was repeated, or a similar question was asked, or follow-up questions were used until the author was satisfied that he had obtained the best and most complete answer possible on the subject covered by the question. In dialect interviews the author used interpreters. At Buldon the interpreter was an ex-Huk EDCOR settler who had been elected secretary of the town council. At Kapatagan the interpreter was not an ex-Huk but was a native of Central Luzon and the president of an important labor union. These interpreters helped immensely in establishing confidence during the interview and in securing free, honest answers.

CHAPTER ELEVEN

[1] José M. Crisol, "Communist Propaganda in the Philippines, 1950–1953," *Philippine Studies,* Vol. 1, No. 3–4, December 1953, p. 209.

INDEX